Christ's battlers

Roger Herft

Bishop of Newcastle

Studies on 2 Corinthians for Lent and other times

APA

Published November 1997
by Anglican Press Australia
PO Box A287, Sydney South, NSW 1235

National Library of Australia
ISBN 1 875861 39 4

Cover art by Jo Sterland

Printed in Australia by Alken Press

A FOREWORD FROM THE PRIMATE

Lent is a time for spiritual stocktaking, so we ought to use it wisely and make the most of it as an opportunity for the refreshment of repentance and growth. Most of us will need some help, and a framework that will give us a discipline and a direction.

Bishop Roger Herft has given us just such a framework: *Christ's Battlers* is a series of studies – one for each day of Lent – which uses Paul's second letter to the Corinthian church as its foundation.

The structure of each small study is familiar enough (a short passage from the text; a brief commentary; a suggested reflective prayer), but with lovely twists of humour and wisdom. Bishop Roger (who is to be Chaplain of the 1998 Lambeth Conference) has added a truly international perspective: adapted extracts from the Lambeth Conference preparatory document give a wider view on issues than perhaps we might have expected. Those who use these studies will, as Bishop Roger hopes, be made more aware of the Lambeth Agenda, and be given an insight into some of the issues with which the bishops will be wrestling.

These are engaging, eminently readable studies in 2 Corinthians, and they will richly repay the effort they exact.

+ Keith Rayner

LAMBETH CONFERENCE 1998

More than 2,000 bishops, priest and laypeople from every part of the Anglican Communion will gather in Canterbury from 18 July to 9 August 1998 for the Lambeth Conference. Established in 1867, the Conference meets every ten years. It is not a legislative body, but it carries great influence. Lambeth reports and resolutions are used in provinces across the world as helpful pointers in matters of faith and order.

The Conference is a celebration of an Anglican Communion that began with all the hallmarks of 'the British Raj abroad' and has become, as Archbishop Desmond Tutu described it, 'the rainbow people of God'.

Bishops have been asked to 'bring their diocese – with its celebration and pain – to the Conference'. The central concerns of the 39 Provinces have been fed into regional meetings, and incorporated into a preparatory document for all participants at the Lambeth Conference.

Bible studies form an integral part of the Conference, as participants gather round the Word of God to share the struggles and joys of ministry and leadership. Bible study coordinator Bishop Simon Barrington-Ward introduces the studies on 2 Corinthians:

> Paul is seeking to resist the expectations of the Corinthians with their intensely competitive, acquisitive and individualistic culture. They want their leaders to be powerfully dominant, big characters. Over and against the pressure of their expectations, Paul wrestles with his own hurt and the temptation to manipulate. He struggles to exercise only the Christ-like authority of a vulnerable and humbled integrity, reflecting the glory of the cross.

Pray that all those who are given the gift of authority will wrestle alongside Paul, to discern and to live out a leadership that is closer to the mind and heart of Jesus.

Lord, by your Spirit and through your word,
make us, with all who lead your people,
so to take up your cross
that we may point others to your resurrection,
so to share your poverty
that we bring others to your riches,
so to bear the mark of your wounds
that we may with others reflect your glory,
so to enter into your death
that we may share with others in your risen life,
and be drawn into the communion of the Triune God
now and forever. Amen.
2 Corinthians 12

ACKNOWLEDGMENTS

I am grateful to all those who have challenged me and continue to strengthen me in my walk with Christ.

This offering would not have come together if not for the wise scholarship on 2 Corinthians by Francis Young and David Ford, Ben Witherington III, Paul Barnett, C.K. Barrett, Peter F. Ellis, Kenneth Bailey, Carol A. Newsham and Sharon H. Ringe, *The Women's Bible Commentary* SPCK, Floyd V. Filson and James Reig, *The Interpreters' Bible Commentary.*

Thanks are due to the Archbishop of Canterbury, the Most Rev. Dr George Carey; Secretary General of the Anglican Consultative Council, Canon John Peterson; Manager of the Lambeth Conference 1998, David Long; Lambeth Conference Secretary, Elizabeth Gordon Clark; and the participants at the St Augustine's Seminar for making available the draft documents for the Lambeth Conference 1998 for adapted use in this book.

I am appreciative of the extensive work done by Ms Barbara Hume, the Bishop's Secretary in the Diocese of Newcastle, in the putting together of this book with its complex format; Canon Dr Ann McElligott, Principal of the St John's College Centre of Ministry, for going over the text and for her helpful suggestions; and my wife Cheryl and the family whose support and encouragement were invaluable.

I am grateful to Belinda Pollard, Theological Editor (APA) for her enthusiasm and devoted care to detail. Thanks to Mamie Long, Publisher (APA) for her kind invitation to me to take on this task and for her unwavering support.

If there is one disappointment for me it was the need to omit prayers from *A Prayer Book for Australia* (Broughton Books, 1995) which were included in the initial draft. They are omitted due to stringent copyright factors and cost restrictions.

I hope this book will help the Anglican Church in Australia and in other parts of the world to prepare effectively for the Lambeth Conference 1998 and for our worship and witness in God's world.

INTRODUCTION

These 47 daily reflections follow the passages from 2 Corinthians selected for the Lambeth Conference 1998. The theme of the Lambeth Conference Bible Study is *Episcopacy under pressure.*

After each reflection, adapted segments from the Lambeth preparatory document are included. They follow the themes of the conference: *Called to full humanity, Called to live and proclaim the Good News, Called to be faithful in a plural world, Called to be one.* The complete document for Lambeth 1998 is available through your local diocese or through the Anglican Communion Office in London.

The meditations found in this book could be used by groups or by individuals for the period from Ash Wednesday to Easter Day. They could also be used for study during the period leading up to and including the Lambeth Conference.

I trust this book helps to meet the Archbishop of Canterbury's desire for the Lambeth Conference:

> I hope that Lambeth 1998 will be supported by all the Communion as the bishops meet in the dying years of the present millennium. Effective leadership depends upon vision, faith and commitment. I believe Lambeth 98 will help to focus the minds and hearts of all bishops as the Anglican Communion prepares for the challenges and opportunities of the new century.
>
> Please support Lambeth 98 and your bishop as he or she prepares to come. Above all remember it in your prayers. I, too, shall draw strength from that support, knowing that it represents our common desire to serve Christ in a world He loves.

It is my hope that, by using this book, people at every level of church life might through study and prayer become aware of the Lambeth Agenda, and contribute constructively towards the discussion and outcome.

+Roger Herft

PAUL AN APOSTLE, TO THE CHURCH OF GOD

Paul, an apostle of Christ Jesus by the will of God, and Timothy our brother, to the church of God that is in Corinth, including all the saints throughout Achaia: Grace to you and peace from God our Father and the Lord Jesus Christ. (2 Corinthians 1:1-2)

Joe, an American Indian, was being shown round the city of New York by Tom who lived there. Tom was proud of the vibrancy of the place with its constant stream of people. Joe suddenly stopped and said to his friend, 'I can hear a cricket chirping.' 'Nonsense! Crickets have not been seen in this city for years,' replied Tom. Moving quickly to the edge of the footpath Joe put his hand into a crevice. There it was – a cricket singing away. 'You must have bionic ears,' remarked Tom. 'No. Watch this.' Taking a coin from his pocket Joe tossed it into the bustling crowd. As soon as the coin hit the ground people stopped and began to look for it. 'See?' remarked Joe. 'You listen to what you love.'

Who or what do our leaders listen to? Leadership at every level in our world is under scrutiny. There is growing suspicion of authority, and it was the same in Paul's time. Dissension was seriously undermining Paul's authority.

Paul and the Corinthians seem to disagree over who he should listen to. Ben Witherington III, in *Conflict and community in Corinth,* says the Corinthians see themselves as Paul's benefactors. They believe Paul should listen to them, but the apostle of God sees it differently.

An apostle is one who is called forth. In some eastern languages to be called forth is to listen, to obey and to act. Paul grounded his leadership in the calling out he received from God in Jesus. God is the source of all apostleship. This calling forth and sending out is the essence of the church. It is not a building or an organisation, but a dynamic act of assembling, and the results of that act. Church refers to what the people of God both do and are.

As a group or as individuals, we authenticate or deny the God who calls us by how we gather and how we act. 'The God you worship,' said Bishop Stephen Neil, 'is portrayed in the life you and I lead.'

A leadership that listens to the God who calls forth is the key for vision.

Eternal God,
you lead us to know you in Jesus.
You are the source of our calling;
be the centre of all our being and doing, through Christ our Lord.

DISCUSSION

What models of leadership does the church offer through its leaders? How do these models enable or hinder us all to listen and act upon God's leading?

LAMBETH 98: Called to live and proclaim the Good News

We believe in a God who calls created beings to a future greater than they could ever make for themselves. From the beginning of the biblical record onwards, the voice of God is active, provoking humans to move and change, to recognise who they are and what - by God's help - they can become. The very name of the church, in Greek, means a community that has been *summoned,* not one that chooses to bring itself into being.

And at the climax of biblical history, 'God sent his Son'. God's very being, beyond the world and its history, is involved in an act of sending. And God the Son, God the Word, appears on earth. His whole existence is a mission: all that he is, is what God speaks and gives; he is God moving towards us, God's voice made into a real human life. As he draws human beings around him in trust and friendship, he equips them in turn to call and communicate through the gift of his Holy Spirit.

Thursday ***Day 2***

BLESSED BE!

Blessed be the God and Father of our Lord Jesus Christ, the Father of mercies and the God of all consolation, who consoles us in all our affliction, so that we may be able to console those who are in any affliction with the consolation with which we ourselves are consoled by God. (2 Corinthians 1:3–4)

When leadership is under question, when the role of the church to lead people into holiness is doubted, how must we react?

Paul was deeply hurt by the words and actions of those who caused strife and questioned his authority. The reputation he had built over years of ministry among the Corinthians was under attack. Paul's leadership as an agent of the gospel brought him much anxiety and emotional strain. His life was linked intrinsically with those who had come to new life by his proclamation of the gospel. Now those he had brought to Christ by this costly love had turned against him.

Paul responded in praise to God. Paul had experienced God's consoling mercy in his affliction. His time of rebellion had brought him face to face with Jesus. He had to answer God's eternal cry from the heart, 'Saul, Saul, why?'

Walter Brugemann, in *The prophetic imagination,* says praise leads to compassion and justice, 'for such songs transfigure fear into energy'.

Paul answered the deep pain of having his credibility questioned in the great Jewish tradition of praise: 'Blessed be God!'

Grant us, O God of consolation, a spirit of praise in our lives that as we grieve for the certainties of the past we may look to you with thankful hearts, for your promise is to be with us forever.

DISCUSSION

What hurts does the church suffer in its witness? What praise can we offer at such a time?

LAMBETH 98: Called to live and proclaim the Good News

To speak of the vulnerable situation of many churches today reminds us that living and sharing in the mission of Jesus may be dangerous. Many Christians live with the immediate risk of violence, harassment, or imprisonment. But all Christians experience risk at some level. For church leaders, it may be the risk of letting go of central control. For congregations, it may be the pain of letting go some treasured way of doing things as the call of Christ is more deeply heard. And there is a risk at a deeper level where we are exposed to hostile spiritual forces. The New Testament speaks in terms of 'spiritual warfare'; with Christ we struggle with the forces of death that seek to enslave and destroy God's world. In the daily exercise of ministry and mission, we must learn to protect one another by prayer, and always to deepen our work of intercession. And we may well thank God for those in intercessory networks and religious vows, who confront the powers of darkness on the church's behalf by their sacrifice of praise, faithfulness and silence.

Friday ***Day 3***

THE SUFFERINGS OF CHRIST

For just as the sufferings of Christ are abundant for us, so also our consolation is abundant through Christ. If we are being afflicted, it is for your consolation and salvation; if we are being consoled, it is for your consolation, which you experience when you patiently endure the same sufferings that we are also suffering. Our hope for you is unshaken; for we know that as you share in our sufferings, so also you share in our consolation. (2 Corinthians 1:5–7)

Leaders are often tempted to share the pessimism of the world and to be cynical about the pain accompanying the daily pressure of being faithful. 'True leadership,' wrote Paul, 'is to identify with the suffering of Christ.'

Christ's sufferings are unique precisely because they are abundant for us today. Christ bore the world's sin, alienation and guilt for all time on the Cross. Christ's redeeming love is abundant for us now. To know consolation, I must first recognise my pain. Only then can I be consoled by Christ who bears that pain. Paul knew this. When Paul experienced separation, the chasm that opened when trust was abused or destroyed, he shared the truth of the Cross. The love that suffered was the love that saved.

It is said when you get to heaven you will be asked only one question, 'Where are your wounds?' If you say you have none, Christ will ask you, 'Did you never love enough to be hurt?' To love is to be wounded. C.S. Lewis wrote in *The four loves*:

> To love at all is to be vulnerable. Love anything and your heart will certainly be wrung and possibly be broken. If you want to make sure of keeping it intact you must give your heart to no one, not even an animal. Wrap it carefully round with hobbies and luxuries; avoid all entanglements; lock it up safe in the casket or coffin of your selfishness. But in that casket, safe, dark, motionless, airless, it will change. It will not be broken, it will become unbreakable, impenetrable, irredeemable. The alternative to tragedy or at least the risk of tragedy is damnation. The only place outside Heaven where you can be perfectly safe from all the dangers and perturbations of love is Hell.

We who are the body of Christ in the world, its members and its leaders, are called to acknowledge our wounds. Covering our wounds only produces cynicism and negativity. Our woundedness points to the Cross, to Christ whose sufferings are sufficient and whose love is gloriously abundant.

Holy God,
in Christ you bore our sufferings, being wounded for us.
Give us a sense of true repentance that, healed by your love,
we may refrain from wounding others.
For Jesus' sake.

DISCUSSION

What wounds do we acknowledge in our local church community? How do we see Christ's sufferings in those wounds?

LAMBETH 98: Called to be faithful in a plural world

Because Christians are called to serve and embody the values and aspirations of the reign of God in their own situation, they are always in tension with whatever culture they call home. Faithful witness requires examining in the light of the reign of God the assumptions and values of that culture, noting that some of them may be evident in the life of the church itself. For Christians, such reflection is part of the ongoing repentance and conversion demanded by the gospel.

The Anglican Communion offers a valuable forum in which that process of reflection and transformation can take place. Dialogue with Christians of other cultures can provide the prophetic challenge to transform whatever might be foreign or even hostile to the values of the gospel. Sharing the stories of God's presence among us in our many contexts can strengthen our faith and give us new insights and courage to sing the Lord's song in our own land.

Pessimism in one cultural context is challenged by hearing of the dynamic and costly witness of Christians in other places. Those who suffer persecution in certain countries are encouraged by the knowledge that other Christians stand by them in prayer and support.

Saturday ***Day 4***

FICKLENESS

I hope you will understand until the end – as you have already understood us in part -- that on the day of the Lord Jesus we are your boast even as you are our boast. Since I was sure of this, I wanted to come to you first, so that you might have a double favour; I wanted to visit you on my way to Macedonia, and to come back to you from Macedonia and have you send me on to Judea. Was I vacillating when I wanted to do this? Do I make my plans according to ordinary human standards, ready to say 'Yes, yes' and 'No, no' at the same time? (2 Corinthians 1:13b–17)

Many call for leadership that is firm, is unbending, and does not vacillate. Many want the church to offer a leadership with absolutes. 'Yes' and 'No'. No shades of grey. It's all there in black and white!

Bishop Paul Barnett comments on this passage in *The message of 2 Corinthians*:

> In popular novels nothing ever goes wrong for the hero. He strides through each episode of the story with success after success. It is not

> like that for ordinary people in real life; it is not like that for Paul. Because he did not return immediately to Corinth, as he indicated he would, the Corinthians now regard Paul as a double-minded man, unable to stick to his plans. One senses in these words of Paul that nothing he can say will be able to change the Corinthians' opinion about him. And yet from his viewpoint he had the best of reasons for changing his plans and honourable motives for doing so.

Paul faced charges of double-mindedness and insincerity in both his words and actions. If ever the foundations of integrity in leadership were shaken, this is it. 'Paul, you cannot be trusted!'

Paul looked into the mirror of his soul – where motives are founded and where the seeds of pride are nurtured. For Paul this mirror bore the perspective of eternity, 'the day of our Lord Jesus'. Here he found God provided a different set of possibilities. Was it possible to believe that their anger at his not coming could have been because they actually cared deeply for him? Paul tested his motives and directions, including his travel plans, in the light of God's purpose for his life.

In *Conflict and community in Corinth,* Ben Witherington III notes that, to those who open their consciences to such burning scrutiny, God gives the gifts of 'simplicity and sincerity'. Authority that is marked by these virtues makes possible a life lived freely, adventurously, and trustingly in the hands of God.

The sin in the Garden of Eden is not that of vacillation. It is the sin of refusing to think for oneself simply and sincerely, and refusing to trust the voice of God on the journey to wholeness.

Merciful God, Mirror of our soul, in Christ you hold up before us our motives for loving you and serving your world. Keep us simple and sincere that we may boast in your love for us, in Jesus our Lord.

DISCUSSION

What questions and issues in life require a 'Yes' or 'No'? How do we deal with the accusation of double-mindedness?

LAMBETH 98: Called to be faithful in a plural world

The Hebrew and Christian Scriptures provide the standard for the Christian church, but they record an enormous variety of expressions of who God is and the behaviour considered to be appropriate responses to God. That diversity of faith is repeated in the formative period of the Christian tradition, and indicates that no one understanding of the mystery of God or prescription of appropriate Christian response can ever be absolute.

A similar diversity is experienced by the member Churches of the Anglican Communion, who are bound to each other by a common spiritual ancestry and the common faith we share. At times, our differing perceptions of the gospel and the many ways in which we seek to be faithful in different contexts may challenge and even impair that communion. But the transcendent nature of the reign of God reminds us that no culture completely embodies the gospel, just as no culture is left without some sign of God's presence.

We can affirm that salvation has been made accessible to all people through Christ. Yet we do not claim that the revelation which Christians have received implies that no other truth about God or creation can be imagined or assumed. To the contrary, the gracefulness of a God who has left witnesses at all times and places should move us to humility. There are limits on our ability to perceive the whole truth about the God of all creation. Relationships between Christians and people of other religions should therefore be founded on mutual respect. They should result in dialogue that searches for common beliefs, acknowledges honest differences, and enables us, wherever possible, to work together in service to the world.

Sunday **Day 5**

THE 'YES' OF GOD

As surely as God is faithful, our word to you has not been 'Yes and No.' For the Son of God, Jesus Christ, whom we proclaimed among you, Silvanus and Timothy and I, was not 'Yes and No'; but in him it is always 'Yes.' For in him every one of God's promises is a 'Yes.' For this reason it is through him that we say the 'Amen,' to the glory of God. (2 Corinthians 1:18–20)

'Quit wasting your energy by playing games on the sidelines – give your full attention to the main event', was the motto of our school rugby coach.

It is so easy to get passionate about little things that have no ultimate bearing on the main purpose of the church. Most of the political games and shrewd jockeying for positions of power that absorb so much energy sidetrack us easily from the gospel.

Paul called the Corinthians to look beyond his frailty and their accusations of his fickleness to see the integrity of the gospel. **It** is the Good News.

The word gospel, meaning Good News, may have derived from a Roman military custom. Slaves were taken with the armies into combat to perform menial tasks. When a battle was won, the commander would call for a herald to take a slave with him to proclaim the victory to the people back home.

The slave who accompanied the herald was granted immediate freedom. When the 'good news' was taken to the city, the cry of the slave had an extra note of triumph and joy – 'the battle has been won and I am free!'

Paul's leadership came from the 'Yes' of God in Christ – the Good News. The battle is won, the Cross proclaims the victory to the world for all time, and I am free.

In Christ, every one of God's promises is a 'Yes'.

Almighty God
give us such a vision of your purpose
and such an assurance of your love and power
that we may ever hold fast the hope
which is in Jesus Christ our Lord.

DISCUSSION

What are the issues that sidetrack us from the main event? How are we in the local church being encouraged to proclaim the Good News, the main event, in our lives and in the world?

LAMBETH 98: Called to live and proclaim the Good News

Our calling is *from* God, the Father, the Source of everything. He calls us out of darkness into the kingdom of his Son and sends us out in the power of the Holy Spirit to live and proclaim the Good News of the kingdom. Our call and our sending does not depend on our resources or lack of them. All are called and all are sent.

This reminds us that we believe in a God who is completely engaged in mission, and whose very life is a movement outwards to give and share divine life and joy. One of the most truly distinctive things about Christian faith is that we believe in a God who has undertaken a mission from all eternity.

So mission is never our invention or choice. It has always started already! We have been caught up in God's own movement of love by being called to be with Jesus. To be with or 'in' Jesus is never to enjoy some private relationship with him; it is to be moving with him – from the heart of God to the ends of the earth. 'As the Father has sent me, so I send you,' says Jesus. And just as *being sent* lies at the centre of who Jesus is, so it does with us as Christians.

Monday **_Day 6_**

WE ARE THE AROMA OF GOD

But thanks be to God, who in Christ always leads us in triumphal procession, and through us spreads in every place the fragrance that comes from knowing him. For we are the aroma of Christ to God among those who are being saved and among those who are perishing; to the one a fragrance from death to death, to the other a fragrance from life to life. Who is sufficient for these things? For we are not peddlers of God's word like so many; but in Christ we speak as persons of sincerity, as persons sent from God and standing in his presence. (2 Corinthians 2:14–17)

Millions of dollars are spent on making people and things 'smell good'. Aromatherapy is a rapidly growing industry, promising to cure ailments and allergies. Perfume manufacturers peddle their wares before the world with salacious advertising campaigns. The aroma of Christ is being similarly hawked with persuasive advertising hype. The 'triumphal procession' has entered the World Wide Web and cyberspace with the intensity of a spiritual Star Wars.

Paul reminds us that the gospel is not a consumer product. The fullness of the gospel cannot be peddled via satellite stations. We do not purchase Christ; we become a captive, a prisoner, held fast in the chains of Christ's love. Our triumphal procession includes a prisoner tied to a cross and a persecutor blinded by the light of grace on the road to Damascus and made fragrant with the aroma of Christ. The captive dragged along in this procession could hardly exude an odour of grace. Think again, says Paul.

The Christian, even despised and rejected, exudes an attractiveness that draws others. Some smell the fresh fragrance of new life, others the odour of a decomposing corpse. Beauty, when it comes in the form of a cross, can be distracting to the closed mind, and mercy can torment a soul more than vengeance!

Holy Jesus, eternal fragrance of God,
you gave up your glory becoming a slave for our sake –
pour out the aroma of your saving grace upon our sinful lives
that the world may inhale again the perfume of your radiant beauty.

DISCUSSION

What scent does Christianity give to the world? How is the aroma of God's holiness present even when the wind seeks to blow against it?

In *The message of 2 Corinthians,* Paul Barnett writes:

> By using technology, is it possible that we Christians become just another depersonalising and alienating force within our community? Moreover, do we not sometimes find the commitment of ourselves as persons to other persons too high a price to pay? It seems easier to deliver 100 church leaflets to letterboxes than to get to know just one person. When we depersonalise the gospel we rob it of its intrinsically human character. How important, therefore, to keep the balance between speaking the Word of God and being the aroma of Christ.

LAMBETH 98: Called to live and proclaim the Good News

One challenge facing the church in the 21st century will be the use of new technologies in proclaiming the faith. Fear of 'televangelism' – which is disconnected from local Christian communities – makes many Christians unwilling to think seriously about the enormous opportunities. New communications media can put people in touch with the gospel and extend information about the church well beyond its membership. In addition to conventional broadcasting, there are openings for interactive learning programmes for the computer, video facilities for large and small scale conferences, and ministry to the house bound. The Anglican Communion works hard to keep abreast of new developments, and we need to think about what is possible in the sphere of new communications technology.

Tuesday ***Day 7***

FREEDOM

Indeed, to this very day whenever Moses is read, a veil lies over their minds; but when one turns to the Lord, the veil is removed. Now the Lord is the Spirit, and where the Spirit of the Lord is, there is freedom. And all of us, with unveiled faces, seeing the glory of the Lord as though reflected in a mirror, are being transformed into the same image from one degree of glory to another; for this comes from the Lord, the Spirit. (2 Corinthians 3:15–18)

Many worship at the shrine of freedom. Economic, political, social, religious freedoms are fought for, lived for, and died for.

In the Academia in Florence one can see some strange blocks of marble called *The Prisoners.* They are said to be the unfinished work of Michaelangelo. From each block of marble, a rough human form seeks to emerge, yet remains captive in the stone.

Paul knew profoundly the agony of being clutched in the power of the Law, the Ordinances and the Covenant of Moses. When he turned to Christ he emerged as a free child of God. True liberty is not doing what we like; it is the power to do as we ought. We are only truly free when our capacities are released through devotion to something greater than ourselves. Being transformed into the likeness of Christ is a journey of prayer, and worship and faith.

Mahatma Gandhi is said to have described Christians as 'ordinary people who make extraordinary claims. If they were more 'Christ-like' one may succumb to their God.'

The challenge that Paul raises for us concerns the 'veil' that is lifted when Christ enters a person's life, and the temptation to 'veil' the gospel of its life-giving power by confining it to the limit of our particular experience. Becoming Christ-like is to be engaged in 'unveiling', in freeing the image of God found in all humanity.

'We are to labour with God, to help God's children become ever more human, which is a glorious destiny,' said Desmond Tutu. In a real sense, none of us is free as long as any person is regarded as less than human, less than a child of God.

Make me a captive to your love, Lord. Then will I be free to love you, become more like you and enable others to be truly free.

DISCUSSION

What are we freed from by the gospel? What are we freed to be and do by the same gospel? How is freedom expressed in leadership? How does our experience of God limit or free the gospel?

LAMBETH 98: Called to full humanity

Racism enforces discrimination on the basis of visible characteristics like race and skin colour. These are unalterable characteristics given by God in Creation. In political terms, racism is about control, exclusion and subjugation. Racism determines *who* has power to make and enforce decisions, and *whose* destiny such decisions affect. It controls access to resources and it sets standards for acceptable behaviour based on the values and cultural system of the dominant group. Racism is a threat to peace. It has to impose its will by violence and it gives rise to resistance and struggle. Racism is an heretical ideology, a false religion. It denies God's intention in creation. Racism distorts human value.

Ethnic identity is a given fact of creation like race, tribe or language. Ethnicity and nationalism are marks of human identity. There is nothing intrinsically wrong with them. Instead they should be joyfully acknowledged and recognised by others. They cause problems, however, when they become sources of vanity and bigotry, when they lead to blind allegiance, or when they become a barrier in our relationships with our neighbours and justify conflict. When that happens, Christians must re-examine their allegiance and remind themselves of the authority of Christ.

Wednesday ***Day 8***

THE VEILED GOD

And even if our gospel is veiled, it is veiled to those who are perishing. In their case the god of this world has blinded the minds of the unbelievers, to keep them from seeing the light of the gospel of the glory of Christ, who is the image of God. (2 Corinthians 4:3–4)

While George Carey, Archbishop of Canterbury, was Bishop of Bath and Wells, he wrote *The great 'God' robbery*. In the introduction to the book he wrote 'Western culture has done us a disservice, it has so robbed us of the sense of the transcendent that we are unable to give due attention to the question of God. Our world is a one-dimensional grey world bereft of mystery, awe and wonder.' Harold Kushner, a Jewish Rabbi, suggests secular culture has a way of extinguishing sacred fires.

The language of faith and personal testimony, of lives changed, of new beginnings, seems snuffed out of modern human consciousness. Caught in the bigotry of rationalism, many perceive anything Christian as superstitious. The decision by Australian jockey Darren Beadman to give up the lucrative racetrack and follow Jesus brought responses of dismay and embarrassment. Virginia Tridi in *The Australian* (9/8/97) explains the problem we face with religious experience:

> Unlike the zealous Pilgrims who stumbled into America's shore seeking freedom of religious expression, Australia's convict ancestors would have preferred a good drink and a gamble and we still do. Hence our Beadman dilemma: a millionaire jockey (riding a horse named Saintly!) gives up a life that thousands of Australians would kill for and turns to the God we turned away from long ago. It stuns us; it positively embarrasses us. Saintly's trainer, Bart Cummings, managed to suggest that Beadman may need a second opinion. In a country where religious apathy is our version of religious tolerance, that's as close to religious persecution as an Australian can get.

The veil to which Paul refers was a blindness brought about by a belief system that adored a former or present glory and refused to see God acting in Christ.

Paul claimed that this lack of perception was difficult to break through, for it had been given the status of a deity by the Corinthian community.

O Saviour Christ,
in whose way of love lies the secret of all life,
and the hope of all people,
we pray for quiet courage to match this hour.
We did not choose to be born or to live in such an age;
but let its problems challenge us,
its discoveries exhilarate us,
its injustices anger us,
its possibilities inspire us
and its vigour renew us for your kingdom's sake. Amen.

DISCUSSION

How can the 'God in whom there is no un-Christlikeness' be unveiled in this age where Christ has been relegated to a swear word? What are the veils that prevent us from hearing the Good News? How can the church unveil the blindness?

LAMBETH 98: Called to live and proclaim the Good News

The gospel is translatable. On the Day of Pentecost, people heard the apostles speaking about God's deeds of power in their own languages. The gospel must be expressed in a voice and in actions recognisable in a culture. But we must not let it be drowned out by voices from the culture that may be present in the church but which are alien to the gospel. This can happen when people insist that religion is a very personal thing and so cloak their reluctance or inability to speak of personal faith in Jesus to others. It can happen when the gospel is presented by using sales techniques rather than by the sacrificial personal engagement that marked the communication of Jesus. It can happen when people present the gospel as an instant solution to all problems and an almost magical route to wealth and prosperity, rather than as a call which will involve taking up the cross. We are called to proclaim the Good News in ways that are faithful to Scripture and have integrity in the culture.

Thursday **Day 9**

PROCLAIMING JESUS CHRIST AS LORD

For we do not proclaim ourselves; we proclaim Jesus Christ as Lord and ourselves as your slaves for Jesus' sake. (2 Corinthians 4:5)

The Decade of Evangelism has brought a renewed focus on proclaiming Jesus Christ as Lord. In the Roman Empire, 'Caesar is Lord' was a central faith statement of Emperor worship. The Emperor was an emanation from the gods. As Lord he was sovereign. All the emblems of power, the marching armies, the social strata, pointed clearly to the god who was in power. The earliest Christian creeds of the church challenged this power with the baptismal statement 'Jesus is Lord'. Jesus calls all who speak in his name to be slaves, servants of the Servant King. This is echoed in a credal hymn in Philippians 2:5–11, which describes how Christ emptied himself and took the form of a slave.

For Paul, proclamation of the gospel far surpassed oratory. His opponents criticised his ability to speak effectively, and suggested their superior debating skills had won the day with some in the Corinthian community. Paul believed proclamation was neither a concept nor a creed, but a living presence that had turned him around. The skill of the orator is not in the eloquence of words but in the attitude of heart and mind – a slave who speaks for his or her master.

Those who proclaim Jesus are the 'slaves'. Their task is to point towards a Person, a message, and an act of God beyond themselves. The prayer on the preacher's lips and heart is always a prayer of offering. Convinced of sin within, the message is spoken as 'one beggar telling another where to find the bread that sustains'. In this Decade of Evangelism, the words of the Greeks in John 12:21: 'Sir, we wish to see Jesus' need to echo in the hearts of all those who would proclaim Jesus as Lord.

**Word of God, sharper than a two-edged sword,
penetrate our lives to expose our secrets
and the world's secret sins;
open us to cleansing and to cure.**

DISCUSSION

How are we in the local church living the challenge of the Decade of Evangelism? How, whom and what do we preach?

LAMBETH 98: Called to live and proclaim the Good News

'Culture is the context in which people find their identity' (Lambeth Conference 1988). Proclamation of the Good News demonstrates and talks about the way the kingdom of God is present now, and how life might change in a community or situation if the kingdom of God were to come in power. Proclamation is seen in the work of a missionary bishop in Northern Nigeria, going into a completely unchurched area to proclaim the Good News of Jesus and call people to follow Him.

It is the suffering of a Christian community as in Sudan, bearing patient witness, loving not its life unto the death, because it is convinced that as 'they carry in the body the death of Jesus, the life of Jesus may be made visible in our bodies' (2 Corinthians 4:10). It is the proclamation of the righteous anger of God at what is happening to abused and abandoned children in our world. 10 million children live on the streets, a million live in forced prostitution, and there are 40 million abortions a year, casting a long shadow over our attitude to the next generation.

It is Christian groups working with the poor for their economic betterment - as a challenge to cultures that tell the poor they are lazy or losers who can expect no justice - and explaining why they bother with such people.

Friday ***Day 10***

LIGHT

For it is the God who said, 'Let light shine out of darkness,' who has shone in our hearts to give the light of the knowledge of the glory of God in the face of Jesus Christ. (2 Corinthians 4:6)

Who is this God whom we preach? All who by word or deed proclaim the reality we call God must attend constantly to this question.

What features does this God have? Which language does God speak? Does God have a nationality, a race, a tribe? Which political party would God vote for? With whom does God travel around?

At one time in Israel's history, God was carried around in the Ark. To lose the Ark was to lose God as well as the battle. The Genesis accounts of creation were officially recorded most probably during the Exile in Babylon when the plaintive question was asked by the psalmist, 'How can we sing the Lord's song in a strange land?' The prophets proclaimed that God is the creator of the universe, the source and sustainer of all life, a difficult message for those who prefer God to wear the local national colours!

Over the centuries, empires have put their stamp on God. Christians have succumbed to this temptation. In the name of the Light of the World, darkness and destruction have been wrought.

To answer his critics, Paul declared that the blinding that brought him to his senses on the road to Damascus was the very light that dawned over the void and darkness when God called the world into being. The very light that was created by God's Word of active command 'Let there be light!' is the light that still shines in the face of Christ. To contain that light in the boundaries of tribe, language or nation is to miss the essence of light.

Eternal God, light of the minds that know you, joy of the hearts that love you, strength of the wills that serve you; grant us so to know you that we may truly love you, and so to love you that we may gladly serve you, now and always.

DISCUSSION

What colour is God? How does the gospel reach out to those of all colours?

LAMBETH 98: Called to be faithful in a plural world

Shortly after the conclusion of the 1998 Lambeth Conference, the whole world will embark on the commemoration of a new millennium. For many, it will be a time of awakened hope for humankind and the earth we share. For others, it will be a time of crisis as the seemingly insurmountable problems faced by the human race continue to take their toll of misery and death. For Christians, it will mark the conclusion of 20 centuries of mission and ministry, and point us both backward towards the One whose birth is the turning point of history and forward towards the yet-to-be-fulfilled promises of God's reign.

Perhaps no generation of Christians has had a clearer sense of the breadth of the differences that can separate peoples from one another. Nor has there ever been a time when the unity of faith we share has been so important for the survival of our witness and the healing of the nations.

The God who made of one blood all the nations that dwell on the face of the earth is the same Lord whose divine Word came to preach peace to those who were far off and to those who were near. In him the whole building is joined together and rises to become a holy temple in the Lord. And in him you too are being built together to become a dwelling in which God lives by his Spirit.

May our unity in faith in the Lord Jesus and our diversity be a source of blessing to the whole earth. Though we are many we all share in the same bread of life.

Saturday **Day 11**

TREASURE

But we have this treasure in clay jars, so that it may be made clear that this extraordinary power belongs to God and does not come from us. (2 Corinthians 4:7)

In Sri Lanka, no gathering begins without lighting the traditional oil lamp. The people light clay jars containing oil and a wick, and the flame is passed around. If the jar is well-made the clay adds a red glow to the light.

Our treasure is the whole event of God in Christ, both in the history of the world and in the life and experience of the individual. St Paul reminded those who prided themselves on their 'superior knowledge' of the gospel that the treasure belonged to God.

This precious treasure is held in human beings who are made of dust; frail clay pots. Dust that is a strange mixture of fear and courage, hate and love, despair and hope. In *The stranger in the wings,* Richard Holloway explains this dilemma succinctly:

> Dust I may be, but troubled dust that dreams, dust that has strange premonitions of transfiguration, of a glory in store, a destiny prepared, an inheritance that one day will be my own... So, my life is stretched out in a painful dialectic between ashes and glory, between weakness and transfiguration.

It is this dust that God breathes on in Creation, giving humanity a desire for eternity. The Good News is that this God takes on our dust, the burning flame in a clay pot that tells out the glory of Christ's love. No pride is possible for the clay jar - only gratitude.

O Lord, sever me from myself that I may be grafted in thee:
May I perish to myself that I may be safe in thee:
May I die to myself that I may live in thee:
May I wither to myself that I may blossom in thee:
May I be emptied of myself that I may abound in thee:
May I be nothing to myself that I may be all in thee. (Erasmus)

DISCUSSION

Clay jars with power from on high! How does this relate to your own journey in the faith?

LAMBETH 98: Called to be faithful in a plural world

In every time and culture, the gospel imperative reminds each of Christ's disciples that 'God, who reconciled us to himself through Jesus Christ, has given us the ministry of reconciliation ... entrusting the message of reconciliation to us. So we are ambassadors for Christ, since God is making his appeal through us'.

God's own purposes are carried forward, however imperfectly, through the church's own mission. As Paul comments, 'we have this treasure in earthen vessels'; nevertheless, the task entrusted to us is to seek, in the words of the Catechism of one of our Provinces, 'to restore all people to unity with God and each other in Christ'.

This is the work of the whole people of God: 'you are a chosen race, a royal priesthood, a holy nation, God's own people, in order that you may proclaim the mighty acts of him who called you out of darkness into his marvellous light. Once you were not a people, but now you are God's people'.

All Christians are members of this people, including those ordained persons who have particular authorised roles 'for building up the body of Christ, until all of us come to the unity of the faith and of the knowledge of the Son of God, to maturity, to the measure of the full stature of Christ.'

While the New Testament and Christian tradition offer many images and models of the church, this particular model of the body of Christ is of special value. It clearly identifies the work of the church with Christ's own ministry, and it helps us appreciate the importance of each member and every form of ministry.

Sunday **_Day 12_**

DYING TO LIVE

We are afflicted in every way, but not crushed; perplexed, but not driven to despair; persecuted, but not forsaken; struck down, but not destroyed; always carrying in the body the death of Jesus, so that the life of Jesus may also be made visible in our bodies. For while we live, we are always being given up to death for Jesus' sake, so that the life of Jesus may be made visible in our mortal flesh. So death is at work in us, but life in you. (2 Corinthians 4:8–12)

Oscar Wilde asserted that in war, Truth is the first casualty. It is said when Christian leaders meet or when churches share their gospel endeavour, Truth is often a casualty.

The consumer-driven culture of our time breeds a gospel of success. It flourishes on the idea that being a Christian means one will never fail and that Christianity is the talisman that keeps one safe from emotional, physical and mental hardship.

Paul questions this gospel of the supermarket in a remarkable set of phrases. Brought to the brink, yet restored, healed and forgiven!

I heard the owl call my name by Margaret Craven is a remarkable story of a young priest who is given three years to live. He is sent into a little village to share their life and to teach the Good News. At one point, the priest and the bishop sit in their boat surveying a rugged inlet:

'Always when I leave the village,' the bishop said slowly, 'I try to define what it means to me, why it sends me back to the world refreshed and confident. Always I fail. It is so simple, it is difficult. When I try to put it into words, it comes out one of those unctuous, over-pious platitudes at which bishops are expected to excel.'

They both laughed.

'But when I reach here and see the great scar where the inlet side shows its bones, for a moment I know.'

'What, my lord?'

'That for me it has always been easier here, where only the fundamentals count, to learn what every man must learn in this world.'

'And that, my lord?'

'Enough of the meaning of life to be ready to die,' and the bishop motioned Mark to start the motor, and they went on.

God grant us life long enough to know it finds its only meaning in loving you and serving others.

DISCUSSION

Where do you see your faith afflicted, perplexed, persecuted, struck down? When do you see it not crushed, driven to despair, forsaken or destroyed?

LAMBETH 98: Called to live and proclaim the Good News

The Holy Spirit recalls and illumines for the disciples the words of Jesus and the meaning of his work. The Holy Spirit empowers disciples to bear witness, by their love for one another, their love for their neighbour and especially for the poor and the outcast, that God has come in Christ, that his kingdom is here. This testimony is meant to be seen in everyday situations. But such events need to be explained. Peter explained the 'event' of the disciples speaking in tongues as due to the gift of the Holy Spirit because Jesus had risen; he explained the healing of the lame man at the temple gate as due to the power of Jesus (Acts 2:32–33, Acts 3:16). He told Christian disciples always to be ready to give a reason for the hope that is in them. Christian proclamation is to explain what God is doing in and through Christian lives and the Christian community, announcing the presence of the kingdom, the time of the Lord's favour.

Monday *Day 13*

A NEW CREATION

So if anyone is in Christ, there is a new creation: everything old has passed away; see, everything has become new! (2 Corinthians 5:17)

God was throwing stars into space, moulding dust and breathing into it. A host of angels were in attendance. One group kept asking 'Why?' They became the philosophers. Another group asked 'How?' Scientists were born through this question. Others asked 'When?' Historians trace their ancestry to this group. Yet others asked 'What for?' and they represented the management sector. Still another group helpfully queried 'How can we help?' Philanthropists, social workers and carers had their roots in that question. Another group asked no questions, but cheered God's activity in constant songs of praise. They were the mystics, the poets, the artists, the dreamers.

This last group reminds us that when God breathed into the dust to create human life, he whispered 'I love you'. The Bible tells the story of how this whisper became a person, Jesus of Nazareth. The life, death and resurrection of this Jesus affects the whole created order.

When someone is in Christ, that person's world view changes. He or she realises that the world itself has changed as a result of Christ's death and resurrection. There is no 'business as usual'.

Physicists say all change is interconnected, using the poetic image of a butterfly flapping its wings in the heart of the Amazon jungle affecting the waves on the beaches of a Pacific island. 'There is joy,' said Jesus, 'among the angels of heaven over one sinner who repents.'

The new creation in Christ is a life-transforming experience that affects all of the world around us and that continues till all things are 'held together' in Christ to eternity.

Creator God,
in the Risen Christ you have given the world a new beginning.
The rainbow of resurrection hope fills the universe,
the waters of death have receded
and you have called your church to be the first fruits of the new creation.
May the Holy Spirit, the dove, bring to all those who believe
the tender leaves of new growth.

DISCUSSION

What vision do you have of 'a new creation'? What would your life and the life of the world look like?

LAMBETH 98: Called to live and proclaim the Good News

To be called into the mission of God in Jesus Christ is to be called to full humanity. We are created in the image of God and true fullness of humanity is found only in Jesus. In him was life - human life in its growth, pain, joy and loss.

Jesus' presence and action are to be searched for and traced in all the variety of human experience - of the child and of the elderly, of the Asian and of the European. Where this varied human tapestry is developing towards its full potential for love and reconciliation, the presence of Jesus is coming more fully into view; mission is going forward.

Called to full humanity

God's only Son was crucified - a scandalous injustice. Human beings are capable of appalling affronts to human dignity, and it is our responsibility to protest against and resist such acts of indignity and inhumanity. The church has a duty to bring a message of hope and trust in God. In Jesus Christ, God has overcome the world but we continue to struggle for the realisation of the values for which Jesus was sacrificed.

Environmental issues are among the most important ethical concerns facing humankind at the end of the second millennium. If we are to sustain God-given life on this planet then we will need to change our attitudes and behaviour. Industrial pollution, deforestation, soil erosion, mineral and fossil fuel depletion, species extinction, overpopulation, over-consumption, and even unregulated tourism and development are having devastating global effects.

The poor of the world often live closest to the results of environmental degradation; the youth of the world will inherit the results of the present degradation. A concern for the environment is closely linked to a concern for justice.

Tuesday ***Day 14***

RECONCILIATION

All this is from God, who reconciled us to himself through Christ, and has given us the ministry of reconciliation; that is, in Christ God was reconciling the world to himself, not counting their trespasses against them, and entrusting the message of reconciliation to us. So we are ambassadors for Christ, since God is making his appeal through us; we entreat you on behalf of Christ, be reconciled to God. For our sake he made him to be sin who knew no sin, so that in him we might become the righteousness of God. (2 Corinthians 5:18–21)

A radio station once asked its listeners to choose the two top songs from the previous ten years that had given them a sense of purpose. The choices were interesting. Both were by Simon and Garfunkel. The second choice was *The sound of silence,* a song about alienation and loneliness. The first choice was *Bridge over troubled waters,* a song celebrating acceptance, friendship and reconciliation. The world thirsts for reconciliation, to bridge the silence that separates.

Baptism, the refreshing sacrament of grace, points us back to our birth. Each of us passes through the waters of the womb to enter into the human community. In baptism we pass through the waters of Christ's death and resurrection to enter a humanity redeemed by God's act of reconciliation. The sign of the Cross, the holy act of redemption, marks us as Christians forever.

To belong to the church is to breathe, with thanks, the intimacy we have with God in Christ. Reconciliation is the life blood of the church. Deacons in the act of servanthood with towel and bowl live out God's binding, healing, unifying life. Significantly, those called to the vocation of presiding at the Eucharist also have authority to absolve and to bless, to forgive and to act out forgiveness. As we are nourished by the life of Christ, broken bread and wine outpoured, so we are healed and forgiven.

The ministry of reconciliation lies at the heart of gospel living. The church, more than any community in the world, must prepare its members to be agents of reconciliation. God invites every person to take the radical step of seeking forgiveness. Here Christ reaches out to provide the strength to live in that reconciled wholeness.

The church in every community must face the scandal of its own deep divisions and must reach out to break down the walls of race, class, gender or nationality that divide peoples.

**Almighty God,
from the beginning of time your Spirit moved over the face of this land. We thank you for its contrasting beauty – the red earth, the blue sky, the drought, the flood, the storm, the stillness.
We give thanks for its diversity of peoples, cultures and languages – for its ancient heritage and pioneering endeavour.
Forgive us for exploiting the earth
and for creating division and poverty.
Help us to be reconciled to you
that we may be agents for your reconciling love –
for Christ's sake.**

DISCUSSION

What are the key issues of conflict in your community? How do you see your task as an agent of reconciliation?

LAMBETH 98: Called to full humanity

The Bible testifies to the unity of human community and to humanity's intrinsic dignity in the eyes of God. Discrimination on the basis of race or colour is a product of human sinfulness.

The New Testament church struggled with the vision of unity between Jews and Gentiles. It was never easy. It led to arguments and disagreements. Jesus told parables about Jews and Samaritans which transcended nationalism. Peter was challenged to realise that 'God treats everyone on the same basis. Whoever worships him and does what is right is acceptable to him, no matter what race he belongs to.' Paul's teaching reverberates with the challenge of commitment to non-discrimination, and the message of John's epistles is unambiguous.

Jesus the redeemer has a universal appeal: 'When I am lifted up from the earth, I will draw everyone to me'. In Matthew 28, Jesus told his disciples to go to 'all peoples everywhere'. Jesus' prayer for unity has continuously inspired the church, 'so that they may be one just as you and I are one'.

As a church, we strive for this biblical community of harmony, of unity in diversity and of affirmation of difference which enriches. We should judge no one by human standards. The church is called to be, in the highest measure possible, an instrument, a sign and a foretaste of the unity of humankind. It is a community we often come close to, but never fully attain, especially in the Eucharist as we break bread together across the barriers of race and class, ethnicity or nationalism. It is a community inspired by the church's teaching on the Trinity, a mutually fulfilling relationship between three distinct and yet united persons of the one Godhead. So also do human beings discover abundant life through their relationships one with another.

Wednesday **_Day 15_**

THE ACCEPTABLE DAY

As we work together with him, we urge you also not to accept the grace of God in vain. For he says, 'At an acceptable time I have listened to you, and on a day of salvation I have helped you.' See, now is the acceptable time; see, now is the day of salvation! We are putting no obstacle in anyone's way, so that no fault may be found with our ministry. (2 Corinthians 6:1–3)

At the top end of the Bishop's gardens in Newcastle is an historic 'lead' tower. When Newcastle was a fledgling port it was used as a beacon to lead ships into the harbour. Early this century one of the churches erected a building right in the path of the beacon, obscuring the light that guided the ships. A new tower had to be constructed closer to the reef because the church had got in the way. There are many ways in which we become hindrances to people accepting God's saving grace.

Dissension and division in the church is one obstacle. People rightly ask, 'How can you tell us about the peace of God when you hate each other?' Christian leaders are often, sadly, the worst examples when it comes to working together for the sake of Christ. Pride, vanity and self seeking cause Christians to vilify others who work for Christ.

Paul's opponents hurl insults and innuendo at him. Paul's response is magnanimous – 'We work together for him'. When we accept

God's grace we are reminded that salvation is not ours to possess and allocate and determine. God's initiative of love gives us this gift.

As we are embraced in the awesome reconciling community of Christ we become aware of how far we fall short as reconcilers. We are challenged to live Christ's forgiveness in our own lives, in the life of the church and in the world.

We must tell out the Good News with urgency. 'Now is the day of salvation.' Our world thrives on the 'Now'. Like children demanding that their needs be satisfied immediately, the world demands the fruits of salvation in the 'Now'. The mystery of salvation passes by as we in the church argue about the intricacy of an article or the shape of a vestment. The waters of the 'Now' world call us to repent. Attacking each other makes the cause weak and our virtues flawed.

Living God,
your Word comes to us in the crying demands
of a world that yearns for peace.
Disturb your church,
so that we may put aside our desire to indulge in
petty factions and divisions
and heed your command to tell out the good news of Jesus to all.

DISCUSSION

What steps are we taking in our local church to work together with other Christians? How can we build on them?

LAMBETH 98: Called to be faithful in a plural world

The credibility of the church can be compromised by its disunity.

> Any evangelism which does not build up good relationships with other Christians in the community must inevitably come under question. Local churches therefore should be encouraged to pray and work together in a cooperative and loving spirit as a sign of witness and of the attractiveness of the face of Jesus Christ: 'see how they love one another'. (The Stuttgart Statement of Evangelism, WCC March 1987)

The struggle to recognise the fullness of the gospel faith in settings different from our own is as old as the Christian church itself. But the particular circumstances of our times call us once again as a Communion to wrestle with our differences as well as to celebrate what unites us.

How can we understand the nature of our faith, and the relationship between faith and the many cultures we represent, so that our witness is truly faithful? How do our differences contribute to our unity and our sense of common identity? How can we embrace our membership in one Communion when our differences seem to threaten our common witness? And how does our experience of unity in diversity affect our discussions and relationships with other people, both those of other Christian churches and of other faiths?

Thursday ***Day 16***

SERVANTS OF GOD

But as servants of God we have commended ourselves in every way: through great endurance, in afflictions, hardships, calamities, beatings, imprisonments, riots, labours, sleepless nights, hunger.
(2 Corinthians 6:4–5)

The reconciling gospel encompasses all of life. It prods the inner recesses of our memory, the carefully closeted guilt, and calls us to be reconciled to Christ, who heals the wounds of our past. It reveals our inner fears and anxieties that express themselves in hostility to others, and in the abuse of power. It calls us to a new freedom in Christ.

The gospel reminds us that to be in Christ is to be a new creation. The Christ-event – in the history of the world and in our own lives – affects the whole world. The environment, the community of the church, and the world with its wounds require our response.

Paul, the battler whom Christ won to his love, reminded the church leaders in Corinth that to be agents of this reconciliation they must share the burdens of those they came to serve. Servants of God must be like the prophet Ezekiel, who sat with the exiles.

Paul had endured great inconvenience, primarily because he wanted to be with the people of God at the edge of life. David Adam says we are in danger of developing a 'midlander' mentality. 'Midlanders' are safe people who have never been lost at sea and avoid the 'cliffs of fall', as the poet Gerald Manly Hopkins described the mind's mountains of grief. We avoid being frontier men and women. We fear being sniped at by our own side if we dare to cross boundaries. Real life takes us to the edge. Borders may be hard to define, but we forever cross into new lands. Frontiers are still exciting places, and we should be encouraged to explore them.

The church, as the reconciling agent in God's world, shares the anguish and injustice of the world, not with a sense of futility, but knowing that Christ's act of redemption is all-embracing. It carries the word of hope and possibility to the world. It can speak an authentic word to the edges and frontiers because it is present there!

Holy God,
grant us the beginning of wisdom and love to cast out every fear:
that we may grow more brave,
more ready to hear,
more ready to obey.

DISCUSSION

How are we confined by a 'midlander' mentality? What are the 'frontiers' in our local community? How are we being called to live on the edge of those boundaries?

LAMBETH 98: Called to live and proclaim the Good News

The Good News addresses many kinds of fears. The Good News to people who seek to base their security and identity in their possessions is that they can be freed from anxiety and the concern for status. By grace they can seek Jesus' kingdom and offer their gifts and skills to work alongside poor people, to experience full humanity with them. They find their meaning in the common life of the kingdom.

The Good News addresses exclusion and humiliation. In India, the caste system denies poor people access to worship; to ready supplies of water or good land; to the market. In developed economies people may be excluded from the market by unemployment and so lose their identity; they are treated as nobodies. The Good News of the gospel is that in Jesus, by grace, those who are no people are called God's people, the image of God, called to be stewards of his creation.

The boredom, frustration and hopelessness that many young people feel is manipulated by political extremists who foster social hatred and even terrorism. The Good News addresses anxiety and meaninglessness.

The Good News addresses our hunger for truth and reality. The media and commercial interests exploit pluralism in the name of freedom and choice. The competition of the market puts more and more pressures on families. The fast-changing products of the market and the media, aimed at youth, distance generations from each other. Many are excluded from the market altogether.

Cities are divided, communities fragmented, and vulnerable young, poor and old people suffer. In the absence of an overarching framework, people seek their individual and communal identity in diverse forms of ethnicity and nationalism.

On the one hand we may genuinely welcome such pluralism as freedom from the uniformity which stifles the rich diversity that God wills in humanity.

On the other hand, we may proclaim that there is only one basis for affirming the individuality of peoples and cultures, and at the same time the possibility of their harmonious interaction in one human story. That is the Good News of the kingdom of God in Jesus, revealed in one particular point in history and spread to all ages and cultures. The Good News breaks down in Jesus' own body the causes of hostility between people and between humanity and their Creator.

The evidence of this is the community of God's people, which is to represent the breaking down of barriers between races, genders and classes in one new humanity.

Friday **Day 17**

THE WEAPON OF RIGHTEOUSNESS

[But as servants of God we have commended ourselves in every way:] by purity, knowledge, patience, kindness, holiness of spirit, genuine love, truthful speech, and the power of God; with the weapons of righteousness for the right hand and for the left. (2 Corinthians 6:6–7)

When I was a child in Sri Lanka, I saw a man assaulted and pushed unconscious into a burning barrel of tar. The only reason for his horrible exit from this world was that he was of another race. As a student during the revolutionary uprising, I saw the bullet-riddled bodies of young people being placed on discarded tyres and set ablaze.

The land of my birth is a land of strange contrasts. It has a peaceful bliss, linked with the Buddhist faith that teaches tolerance and compassion. It has a volatility that is menacing and disturbing.

This heritage frightens me, for it exposes a truth about myself that I do not want to hear. I am capable, given a set of circumstances, of acting out the deepest aggression in the most despicable way.

Paul's response to the Corinthians was a mixture of affection, gentle persuading, and bitter, ironic comment. The two natures warring within him are painfully apparent. In this passage, he called upon the church to commend itself in ways that would enable a nobler spirit to win out. The weapons of this contest were the weapons of righteousness, the qualities that promoted human dignity, equality, justice and wholeness.

One tragic fact of our modern world is our dependence on weapons that enhance the aggressive nature within us, allowing us to kill with enormous efficiency.

The prophet Isaiah reminds us that we have a choice when we take up weapons. We can resort to weapons that are as lethal and destructive as those of our enemies, or we can, by God's power, transform them into instruments of common investment for the future – into ploughshares!

God of justice,
you chose an instrument of death, the Cross,
to bring life to the world.
In the confusion and conflict of our daily lives
help us to choose always to use the weapon of costly love,
for it leads to you.

DISCUSSION

How are we dependent on the weapons of death in our daily lives? How can we find freedom to beat our weapons into ploughshares?

LAMBETH 98: Called to full humanity

One factor lying at the root of the problems in the global economy is corruption and militarism. Some national credit agreements, made to finance the purchase of goods and services from creditor nations, are not innocent. They provide a facility for corrupt and despotic leaders to trade in arms from Western arms manufacturers, in order to engage in wars they cannot afford, disturb the peace of neighbouring nations and oppress opposition within their own countries.

In situations of conflict, military expenditure bills, loss of lives and skills, direct damage to property and productive facilities, and disruption to education and economic life all have a devastating effect on the economy.

A military culture inevitably breeds corruption and abuse of power. It feeds on human rights' violations, it is an excuse for suspending democratic rights and civil liberties and it makes governments unaccountable.

Saturday **Day 18**

IMPOSTORS YET TRUE

[But as servants of God we have commended ourselves in every way:] truthful speech, and the power of God; with the weapons of righteousness for the right hand and for the left; in honour and dishonour, in ill repute and good repute. We are treated as impostors, and yet are true; as unknown, and yet are well known; as dying, and see – we are alive; as punished, and yet not killed; as sorrowful, yet always rejoicing; as poor, yet making many rich; as having nothing, and yet possessing everything. (2 Corinthians 6:7–10)

A constant criticism of the Christian community, both from within and without, is that we are hypocrites. Individuals and groups are tempted to live according to public opinion. Malcolm Muggeridge reminds us that only dead fish float with the current. The live ones learn to swim against it.

We find comfort in moving along with the latest trends. Peer pressure is not limited to any generation. All of us succumb to acting in ways that are false and purposeless. The church is not a museum for saints, but a place of hospitality for sinners.

Paul faced criticism from his opponents, who saw him as a liar. He said he would come but he did not; he had no real authority because he was not 'one of the twelve'. He had suffered both mentally and physically; he had worked for his living, refusing the patronage of the elite in Corinth; and he was accused of being powerless and empty.

Paul acknowledged the criticism, and sought to move behind the hurtful weapons of their words. He sought to establish a relationship of love. In *The stranger in the wings,* Richard Holloway describes this condition:

> So, we are caught in a painful tension between a searing, angry, judging ethics of glory and holiness, filled with the true vision of what ought to be; and a wistful, pitiful, pragmatic ethics of dust, rendered hesitant by an overwhelming awareness of what is. Glory and ashes; the end and the beginning; then and now. How can we resolve it, live with it, be one church, one person, when this tension tears us apart?

To live in the here and now with imperfection when one has experienced wholeness with Jesus is frustrating. To know that every move and motive has hypocrisy etched into it is humbling. Paul was aware of this paradox – 'Who will deliver me, wretched man that I am' he cries. The answer comes not with the perfect score in right living but in the knowledge that God shares this frustration for our sake – Jesus who becomes nothing in order that we may possess everything.

Who am I? ...
Am I one person today and tomorrow another?
Am I both at once? A hypocrite before others and before myself,
a contemptible, woebegone, weakling?
Or is something within me, still like a beaten army fleeing in
disorder from victory already achieved?
Whoever I am, thou knowest O God! I am thine!

(Dietrich Bonhoeffer, *Letters and papers from prison*)

DISCUSSION

How do we move beyond condemning the hypocrisy of others to confront our own failings? How do we find strength to swim against the current?

LAMBETH 98: Called to live and proclaim the Good News

The Christian community that lives out its mission in reaching towards the excluded, the poor and the forgotten, will be a community of *covenant* and a community of *hope.*

It promises a stable, nurturing life together, patiently listening to and learning from each other. It reveals a God who keeps promises and will be with us always, who seals his covenant with us in the blood of Jesus.

A living church is one that is journeying towards a fuller representation of covenant faithfulness, one that trains its people to be loyal to each other in all kinds of ways.

In the Base Communities of Latin America, this faithful learning together seeks to equip people for witness and action, to understand their situation and find the power to change what can be changed. The church in South East Asia uses cell groups as the mission frontier of the church. Inquirers and new converts are pastored and nurtured by a group before they are introduced into the full life of the larger congregation.

A living church will nurture covenanted relationships in the family – husband and wife, children and parents, learning how to listen to each other and grow with each other. It will promote commitment to the work of mission. It will encourage people to stay with each other in a congregation, even when there are tensions and disagreements. It will make it possible for people to live through failure because they hold up to each other the promise of Christ's forgiveness.

Thus the church's faithfulness in love is always the ground of hope. Lostness or failure is never allowed to be the last word. A group of Christians failing, quarrelling, grieving, frustrated, yet still standing with each other and hearing one another, bears witness to life triumphing over death.

Sunday **_Day 19_**

OPEN WIDE YOUR HEARTS

We have spoken frankly to you Corinthians; our heart is wide open to you. There is no restriction in our affections, but only in yours. In return – I speak as to children – open wide your hearts also.
(2 Corinthians 6:11–13)

A pop song by Cliff Richard that won a gold disk award was *It's so funny we don't talk any more*. Communication is a strange process. Channels must be open for the message to get through. The opposite of communication is not silence, but alienation and separateness.

Paul had approached the Corinthians using rhetorical skills learned in Jewish and Greek debating schools. He endeavoured to reconstruct his character and name that had been maligned by the people of Corinth.

In (mostly) gentle tones, he wrote to them about what it meant to belong to the church, to that assembly called out by God to reflect in its very character the true nature of God. He bared his soul to them and, in the process, expressed his anguish of their broken relationship. He felt a deep loss, for he had been their parent in the gospel, the sage and elder through whom they had come to know the eternal wisdom of God, even Jesus Christ. Now others had usurped that position.

Paul cried out from the depths of his heart the torment that he felt over their severed communication. The pathos is tangible. It is a cry from a parent to a child. How will the child respond?

God cries for us. God's heart has been opened scandalously on the Cross. God cries for all that has been hidden, broken, impaired in our lives. The tears of God give us permission to cry, too.

The 'cry of the child in the street' was a sign for Isaiah that the vision of God's *shalom* (peace and harmony) was not present. We in the church are often deaf to the cry of the next generation. We have closed our ears to the sound of their crying. The cry of the child suffering neglect and violence, abuse and anger, is for us a festering wound of shame.

Paul's tenderness mirrors the tenderness of God for all creation. Tears can open the gates of communication to the world of pain. They can enfold the stolen children of indigenous Australians, and the children whose innocence is stolen in homes, the very places where shelter and security should be guaranteed.

To ignore this cry is to refuse to wipe the tears of God.

Give us, we pray you gentle God, a mind forgetful of past injury,
a will to seek the good of others and a heart of love.
Grant us, Jesus, that tender, indestructible love which asks
forgiveness for its executioners
and gives hope to the thief on the cross.
Keep us compassionate when the way is hard,
and gentle with those who oppose us.

DISCUSSION

Who in the world of our local church is crying? Whose cries are we ignoring?

LAMBETH 98: Called to full humanity

A Lambeth Conference cannot lay down guidelines about what all churches should be doing in every place. But it can assert on behalf of all that no part of human life is excluded from God's care and concern. It can reaffirm moral principles for the guidance of communities and peoples, as well as for individuals. It can remind the world that there is much to be concerned about in the way human beings hurt each other and exploit God's creation. It can go on asserting, in the face of so much which seems to deny it, that the reconciling power of Christ's love and the motivating power of the Holy Spirit are available to heal, restore and renew a world in which we are promised that 'sin shall not have dominion over you'.

Called to live and proclaim the Good News

The Good News addresses the exploitation of the vulnerable. Street children are dehumanised very early in life due to the increasing wickedness of the adult world. What was designed by God to house the Holy Spirit becomes instead a den of robbers and rapists. Such children know nothing of the childhood God intended. All they know is a collapsed and distorted world of slave labour, sexual abuse and violence.

> Love compelled Jesus to intervene, rescue and protect what is sacred and central to God. Today childhood is bought and sold. In India the church's Council for Child and Youth Care cares for HIV positive children and AIDS orphans with care, rehabilitation and community support. (The Bangalore Statement on Children at High Risk 1997)

The challenge to the church comes not only from such extreme situations but also from children who recognise transcendence. Lest that sense be stifled, they need to experience the welcome of the kingdom of God. This is Good News.

Monday ***Day 20***

MOURNING

For even when we came into Macedonia, our bodies had no rest, but we were afflicted in every way – disputes without and fears within. But God, who consoles the downcast, consoled us by the arrival of Titus, and not only by his coming, but also by the consolation with which he was consoled about you, as he told us of your longing, your mourning, your zeal for me, so that I rejoiced still more. (2 Corinthians 7:5–7)

Often in our Christian pilgrimage we arrive at some point hoping for assurance and stability. Instead we find our 'resting place' to be only a furnace of conflict.

Paul had set off for Macedonia hoping that Titus, his companion, would join him on the journey with news from Corinth. There was no Titus and no news. He described his state of affliction as 'disputes without and fears within'.

Waiting has its own pain. 'Mourning' in Aramaic means 'having a deep longing for something to happen'. Fear feeds on the anxious state, creating demons where none exist. Titus finally arrived safe and well, and the news from Corinth was better than hoped for. The relationship with Paul had not lost its intensity.

Christians throughout the centuries have sought resting places. But they have found living for Christ in the world includes facing the anxiety of waiting, and facing the fear of questions too dangerous to be raised.

The church today is facing many turbulent dilemmas, teetering precariously between life and death. While the abortion debate has become polarised between pro-life and pro-choice absolutes, debates about euthanasia are characteristically about 'crossing lines' or about 'slippery slopes'.

Christians are called to live with such difficult dilemmas, even while we are a community which celebrates life and points beyond death.

O God,
you know our innermost fears,
the doubts, anxiety and uncertainty that face us
in these perplexing times.
Help us to make our decisions trusting in you one step at a time,
so that we may keep to your way and do your will.

DISCUSSION

What dilemmas are most critical for our local community? How do we pray in the midst of a dilemma where we are caught between life and death?

LAMBETH 98: Called to full humanity

Recent technology makes medical ethics increasingly complex. It is possible to keep people with severe disabilities alive for much longer. While this might often be thought highly desirable, it also makes possible some highly distressing cases.

Bishops need to show a mixture of pastoral concern and wise

caution. Euthanasia in its various forms involves people at their most vulnerable. The dangers of marginalising theological considerations are real. Yet so are the fears that one day we ourselves may be suspended between life and death. However protective we are of permanent vegetative state patients, few of us wish this to happen to ourselves.

It is care, not the automatic relief of pain, which is central to pastoral theology in this area. Christ is seen to identify with our sufferings but not always to relieve us of suffering. In Christ we believe we can see meaning and value beyond our sufferings, even if we cannot always see meaning and value within these sufferings. This is not to welcome pain and suffering, but it is to be guided by the belief that their instant relief is not in itself the highest good.

For the Christian, this is not the only life and there is no requirement to prolong it needlessly. Life perceived as God-given is always to be treated with respect, with gratitude and with responsibility. While such a perception might make most Christians cautious about sanctioning the deliberate taking of life, it might also discourage them from clinging pointlessly to it.

The 1996 *Washington Report* observes:

> Paradoxically, those Christians who accept and those who reject assisted suicide and euthanasia begin with similar convictions. Both have a sense of the sovereignty of God. Both want to protect human dignity and to preserve the freedom of individual persons to choose how to confront human finitude and death. They view life as a gift that is good, but not entirely at the disposal of humanity ... They recognise that human life, especially in situations of death and dying, often confronts us with a conflict of goods in which physical life clashes with other purposes or goods of life. Moreover, they are aware that advances in medical technology may be used to preserve and extend life apart from other goods in human life. They agree that among the goals of medicine are those to relieve suffering and restore health, not simply to extend physical life.

Tuesday **Day 21**

GODLY GRIEF

For even if I made you sorry with my letter, I do not regret it (though I did regret it, for I see that I grieved you with that letter, though only briefly). Now I rejoice, not because you were grieved, but because your grief led to repentance; for you felt a godly grief, so that you were not harmed in any way by us. For godly grief produces a repentance that leads to salvation and brings no regret, but worldly grief produces death. (2 Corinthians 7:8-10)

The Hollywood movie *Love story* had as its theme: 'Love means never having to say you're sorry'. We often avoid acknowledging actions that bring pain to others by making excuses. It may be a biological deficiency, 'in the genes'. There may be sociological factors, such as a dysfunctional family. Or it might be psychological weakness – 'they experienced trauma as children'. These may explain behaviour, but they do little to heal the pain.

Worldly grief sees the symptoms – a hurtful word, money owed, an insult handed out – and seeks to rectify the relationship by dealing with the symptom. Keeping your distance becomes the best policy.

Godly grief enables a new beginning. It was established deep in the Hebrew tradition. In the Exodus event, the grieving and groaning enables a movement of spirit from numbness and false idols that do not hear, to the God who enables us to recognise our hurts and to deal with them. The amazing truth Israel discovers about this God is that Yahweh is present in their grieving. His love brings on sorrow, allowing a change that brings forth renewal.

Paul could have chosen to ignore the hurt. Instead he decided to confront it.

Bishop Michael Malone, the Roman Catholic Bishop of Maitland-Newcastle, preached at the Anglican Synod Eucharist in Newcastle for its Sesquicentenary year. After the Eucharist he remarked that the living encounter of worshipping with Anglicans had brought him grief. He recognised that, as a Roman Catholic, the rules forbade him to receive the Holy Sacrament from Anglicans. So near, yet so far.

The closer we walk together, the more we recognise our common purpose and path in holiness. Division becomes more painful. Work for healing and unity takes on urgency.

**Almighty God,
to whom all hearts are open, all desires known
and from whom no secrets are hidden,
cleanse the thoughts of our hearts
by the inspiration of your Holy Spirit
that we may perfectly love you
and worthily magnify your holy name
through Jesus Christ our Lord.**

DISCUSSION

How are we diminished by the hurt we cause others? How do we know the healing of acknowledging our brokenness?

LAMBETH 98: Called to be one

The road to visible unity is by stages. Throughout history, Christian divisions have developed gradually and untidily. We should not expect the healing of these divisions to happen all at once.

But care is needed to avoid blatant contradictions and blind alleys. An essential part of our work is to review the steps towards unity taken in various parts of the world. Do they hold together and are they compatible with the goal? Such an activity contributes to the transformation of life. It also belongs to that care for unity which is an essential part of the ministry of the bishop, a duty (in the words of Pope John Paul II) 'which derives directly from fidelity to Christ, the Shepherd of the church'.

Wednesday ***Day 22***

REQUESTING

Now as you excel in everything - in faith, in speech, in knowledge, in utmost eagerness, and in our love for you - so we want you to excel also in this generous undertaking. (2 Corinthians 8:7)

Sevak Selvaratnam, known as the Elder Brother in Sri Lanka's monastic ashrams, told how he had been challenged to experience God's liberality.

On one occasion, when gifts were being received, a couple came forward, tears streaming down their cheeks, and placed on the offertory plate two gold bracelets. After the service he rushed to meet with them, anxious to know the reason both for their tears and for the strange gift they had made.

The couple came from a poor area in the city. They had come to the ashram more than seven years previously and had prayed for a child. A daughter had been born. Selling what they had, they had bought her two gold bangles to remind her that she was circled by the hands of God. A few months before, she had taken ill and died. They had come to give thanks and to offer the gold bracelets to God. Their daughter's life had come from God. Their love for their child came from God. Now the circle was completed in their offering of thanks.

The early church arranged for the poor in Jerusalem to be cared for by the gentile churches. But this offering was not easily organised or sustained. In Corinth it had encountered some resistance. Titus had brought news that some money might be raised for those in need in Jerusalem. Paul called upon the Corinthians to excel in the act of liberality. Their eagerness to share in this endeavour would speak much more powerfully of their faith than any oratory or knowledge.

O God whose love is portrayed to the world in costly giving,
create in us anew that generosity of spirit,
that we may give to those in need freely, lovingly, joyfully.

DISCUSSION

How are we called to exercise generosity? How can generosity with our money allow us to avoid giving of our ourselves? How are we numbed by the enormity of the world's need? Where do we begin?

LAMBETH 98: Called to full humanity

The alarming fact is that despite higher levels of international cooperation since the establishment of the World Bank and the IMF 50 years ago, populations of the developing world are now sliding into a spiral of increasing poverty. The gap between the rich and poor is widening; the richest fifth of the world's people had 60 times more income than the poorest fifth in 1991, up from 30 times in 1960.

Development agencies allege that debt repayments contribute

heavily to this tragedy of escalating poverty. The 1996 Oxfam Briefing Report states that it would be possible by the year 2000 to make social investments which would save the lives of around 21 million African children and provide 90 million girls with primary education, for less than is currently being spent on servicing international debt.

The poor countries of the world are making interest payments which have escalated well beyond what could have been anticipated at the time when the loan agreement was entered into.

The amount of the original capital loan, in most instances, was paid off. But interest payments have accumulated, and the sum still owing has risen. In order to keep paying them, debtor nations find they have to borrow more. It is a vicious spiral which amounts to a new form of slavery.

Thursday **Day 23**

GENEROSITY

I do not say this as a command, but I am testing the genuineness of your love against the earnestness of others. For you know the generous act of our Lord Jesus Christ, that though he was rich, yet for your sakes he became poor, so that by his poverty you might become rich.
(2 Corinthians 8:8–9)

The economy seems to be the determining force in the world today. The indices flashing across our television screens are the modern barometer of whether we are healthy or not. A drop in one sector causes a domino effect across the world. The closing of a steel plant in Newcastle costing the community 2000 jobs makes the 'health indicator' in our society – the share market – rise by as much as 65¢. Social pain produces economic health! If profit depends on human sacrifice, then we have a malaise that eats at the very fibre of our social structure.

St Paul placed the matter of a collection for the poor squarely within the realms of faith and belief in Jesus.

In *Meaning and truth in 2 Corinthians,* Frances Young and David Ford describe the economy of God as bound to the Jesus event:

> Paul's gospel has led him to speak of God in relation to Jesus Christ and the events of his crucifixion and resurrection in such a way that his concept of God is transformed. God and Jesus Christ are spoken of as intrinsic to each other ...
>
> To put it starkly if Christ is 'the image of God', and Christ was weak, poor, 'made into sin', and dead, then we must try to think the almost unthinkable. The relationship of God's very being and glory to weakness, poverty, sin and death must be rethought.

Debt, credit ratings, interest, profit and loss are not entities that are outside the scope of the God/Jesus revelation. The truth it portrays is that the economy of God is not that of the market place. God's economy reconciles wealth and poverty. God's economy redeems the poor and gives true wealth to the rich.

Believing in the Cross, in Jesus' redemption of my life, has economic significance. One of the churches I served in, in Sri Lanka, was named Christ the Healing Saviour. In the centre of the altar was a cross with the words written above 'Tell me what your faith costs you and I will tell you how much it is worth'.

It has been suggested that the real worth of a person's commitment to Christ is not to be found in the knowledge of the Scriptures or their genuflections before the Blessed Sacrament, but in the 'giving' reflected on his or her cheque butts!

Jesus Christ,
you have taught us that what we do to each other, we do to you;
make us quick to help and slow to hurt, knowing that in our neighbour it is you who receive our love or our neglect.

DISCUSSION

Are we prepared to confront the poverty of Christ? Are we prepared to become poor like Christ for the sake of the disenfranchised ones of the world?

LAMBETH 98: Called to full humanity

All the Provinces of the Anglican Communion placed the issue of International Debt as a matter for urgent discussion at Lambeth Conference 1998. This is a measure of the economic crisis that engulfs many developing and underdeveloped countries of the world on the eve of a new millennium.

The reason is not very difficult to understand. A recent World Bank Report states that in 1995, 1.3 billion people in the developing world still struggle to survive on less than $1 per day and the number continually increases. Every year 8 million children die of diseases linked to impure water and air pollution, 50 million children are mentally and physically damaged because of poor nutrition and 130 million children (80% of them girls) are denied the chance to go to school. At the same time one-fifth of the world's population enjoys 85% of the world's income.

Friday **Day 24**

ACT OUT OF COMMON GRACE

And in this matter I am giving my advice: it is appropriate for you who began last year not only to do something but even to desire to do something – now finish doing it, so that your eagerness may be matched by completing it according to your means. (2 Corinthians 8:10–11)

Once a man ended up in hell. Here he found a lavish banquet with every conceivable food. But the people had been given six-foot long chop sticks. (Yes, there are Chinese implements in heaven!) All were angry and miserable for they could get no food to their mouths with these enormous chop sticks. Incensed with this ridiculous situation, he asked the angel if heaven was different. 'Come and have a peek,' suggested the angel. Looking into heaven the man saw the banquet. Everyone seemed contented. 'Have they eaten?' he enquired. 'Yes,' said the angel. 'They must have different chopsticks.' 'No,' answered the angel. 'Those who get to heaven have learned to feed one another.'

The Council of Jerusalem had acknowledged the mutual partnership of all the churches, and Jerusalem required particular attention because of the difficulties it faced. The principle was clear. If one suffers, all suffer. The church agreed that God's face was mirrored in Jesus Christ and that the church, as the body of Christ, was to mirror his self-giving. There was, however, a huge chasm between theory and reality. Paul urged the Corinthian community to move from a desire, a hope that it might happen, to actually complete the task of giving according to their means.

God of all the earth,
you have given us the heritage of this good and fertile land;
grant that we may so respect and use it
that others may thank us for what we leave to them.

DISCUSSION

How is our local congregation enriched and 'fed' by being part of a worldwide Communion? How are we attending to the hunger and needs of others? How are we stewards of God's creation?

LAMBETH 98: Called to full humanity

Economics is a matter of life. The original Greek word means 'the law of the household'. Management of the household ensures that the land may 'enjoy prosperity' and 'experience righteousness' (Psalm 72:3). Christians cannot avoid economic issues. The World Council of Churches' Study on Economic Life, *Christian Faith and the World Economy 1992,* makes an impregnable case for Christian people and churches to be involved in the economic debate and the formation of economic policy.

Christians have a duty to manage the resources of creation, preserve their renewable capacity, meet the requirements of life for those in need and share with the destitute and poor.

The health of the natural order must be preserved and the environment sustained. Rabid consumerism must be restrained and production kept at sustainable levels. Christians must view with the utmost suspicion arrangements whereby production is curtailed in order to increase demand and raise prices. Where economic actors, such as Western banks and donors, find that their use of resources has led to poverty, good stewardship requires that they respond.

Economic theory and practice are morally sustainable only if they promote the justice of God and the wellbeing of humanity. God, who in Jesus Christ came to tabernacle among us and took our nature upon him, calls humankind to care for one another and to bear one another's burdens.

Saturday **Day 25**

CHEERFUL GIVING – GOD'S ECONOMY

The point is this: the one who sows sparingly will also reap sparingly, and the one who sows bountifully will also reap bountifully. Each of you must give as you have made up your mind, not reluctantly or under compulsion, for God loves a cheerful giver. And God is able to provide you with every blessing in abundance, so that by always having enough of everything, you may share abundantly in every good work. (2 Corinthians 9:6–8)

At the height of the British Empire, a man described by a British Prime Minister as a 'half naked fakir from the East' protested against the inequalities of Indian Society. Gandhi suggested that 'world resources were more than enough for all those in need, but not enough to satisfy greed'.

Paul takes the economy seriously. As a tentmaker he worked side by side with business managers and slaves.

Most economies are characterised by how they cope with scarcity. The pre-industrial economy of Paul's time could be described as a 'limited goods' economy. The elite, who took no part in production but exacted taxes and maintained order, comprised 2% of the population. The remaining 98% were engaged in manual work, mainly handicraft manufacturing. There was a stable, limited amount of resources. More for one meant less for others. Unlike our industrial economy with its capacity to generate wealth, there was no way to increase the 'cake' being divided among all. The minority elite dominated the rest of the population, including Paul. Most goods were in short supply.

Subsistence with stability was the aim of economic activity for most people. The right to subsistence was closely bound to one's family and its inherited place in society. It was an economy in which equilibrium, not growth, was the ideal. The economy was supported by a network of relationships based on informal reciprocity, enforced by the powerful appeal to honour and shame.

In *Meaning and truth in 2 Corinthians,* Frances Young and David Ford state that this picture radically contrasts with the divine economy described by Paul. Paul describes an economy characterised by abundance, blessing and generosity.

Paul places the stewardship of our resources within the context of God's economy of abundance. The gift God has given is so boundless that we who are recipients of that grace must act with generosity.

In our own time the church is called to forgive debt, using the Hebrew concept of Jubilee. This will challenge each community of faith to reconsider God's bounty and our responsibility.

Awesome God,
the heavens are filled with your majesty,
yet you chose to reveal your glory
to a people bound in the chains of slavery.
In your Son Jesus Christ

you lived among the outcast and the downtrodden.
Help us to stand with you alongside the poor
until justice cascades from the places that have plenty,
and righteousness becomes an everflowing stream.

DISCUSSION

How does God's economy of abundance shape the life of our local community? Is generosity a scarce commodity?

LAMBETH 98: Called to full humanity

The call for the remission of debt has strong biblical authority. The Book of Leviticus regulates that in the Promised Land people must order their society afresh in keeping with the holiness of the God who is tabernacled in their midst. It was considered a holy thing to limit gains the rich could make at the cost of the poor and indebted.

During the Jubilee Year, balances in nature and in human relations had to be restored. The justification was personal freedom, respect for the integrity of creation and economic rehabilitation. These values of returning land and cancelling debt could be adapted to our situation in response to the devastation and human breakdown we are experiencing.

As we approach the end of the millennium, it is fitting that the developed world be challenged to cancel debt, to allow the poor nations of the world to make a fresh start. This is the Year of Jubilee. For those in debt, this will be an occasion to experience the redeeming love first offered by Jesus on the Cross.

For the creditors of the world, it will be the lifting of the burden of guilt and the offering of sacrificial love in true brotherhood of humanity.

There are three compelling reasons for the cancellation of international debt. One is a moral imperative. No community with a claim to civilised values should tolerate an unpayable debt burden in its midst, with the evils of mass malnutrition, disease and illiteracy. By making the most basic rights and opportunities available to poor people, debt relief could help correct some of the glaring deficiencies in human progress as we near the end of the 20th century.

Second there is the economic argument. Debt reduction will release the productive potential of marginalised communities and help create a framework for more self-reliant growth.

Third is the argument of prudence: it is not in the long-term interests of the world, and certainly not of the richer countries, that so many people are pauperised.

Sunday **Day 26**

GENTLENESS

I myself, Paul, appeal to you by the meekness and gentleness of Christ – I who am humble when face to face with you, but bold toward you when I am away! (2 Corinthians 10:1)

Paul's opponents got under his skin by making their attacks personal. They had suggested that he was humble, not in a virtuous sense, but in being a person of no consequence in face-to-face meeting. In both Greek and Hebrew culture, humility was seen as a weakness, a state of servitude. Distance, said his opponents, seemed to give Paul courage. He was a coward!

Paul responded to the personal attacks by placing his appeal before the Corinthian community, pleading with them to consider the meekness, the gentleness of Christ.

Neil Douglas-Klotz, in *Prayer of the cosmos,* translates the Beatitude 'Blessed are the meek for they shall inherit the earth' from the Aramaic to read:

> Healthy are those who have softened what is rigid within; they shall receive physical vigour and strength from the universe.
> Aligned with the One are the humble, those submitted to God's will; they shall be gifted with the productivity of the earth.
> Healed are those who have wept inwardly with the pain of repressed desire; they shall be renewed in sympathy with nature.
> Integrated, resisting corruption are those who have dissolved heavy morality within; they shall be open to receive the splendour of earth's fruits.

Gentleness and meekness are divine qualities for they allow insults to be absorbed, not with submissiveness, but with active forgiveness. When the victim forgives, when the lamb is slain, when Jesus the innocent one dies, then the appeal is made to all who would listen, the Crucified is the Exalted One.

The ministry of meekness has a particular place in the life of the church in the order of Deacon. To search and to serve is the precious gift the deacon brings to the people of God. In modelling meekness, the deacon calls the whole church to the ministry of the strong, gentle Christ.

Give us, O God, gentle hearts and quiet minds
that can absorb personal insult,
for in Christ you give us the gift of the love that overcomes all.

DISCUSSION

How do the gospel values of meekness and gentleness conflict with the values of the world? How can we live with humility?

LAMBETH 98: Called to be faithful in a plural world

The ministry of service and proclamation of the Word, traditionally associated with deacons, belongs to the whole people. Where deacons exercise their special ministry within the church, they do so by illuminating and holding up the servant ministry of the whole church and calling all its members to that ministry.

Issues of diversity as the church relates to and serves the culture in which it lives are particularly relevant to the order of Deacons, the diaconate.

While all the churches of the Anglican Communion embrace servant-ministry as an integral part of their life together, not all have chosen to restore the diaconate to its more traditional form. In some places, specialised lay roles, such as the lay reader or catechist, may exercise similar functions on the local level.

Hence, renewed attention to deacons also raises questions about their relationship to the church and the other orders. While deacons have traditionally been responsible directly to the bishop, the nature of their ministry often places them at the intersection between the church and the broader society in which they serve.

The last Lambeth Conference commended to the Provinces a review of member churches' ordinals and canons in order to learn about the ministry of a distinctive and permanent diaconate. The 1998 Lambeth Conference provides the opportunity to carry on our reflection about the ministry of deacons in different contexts within the Anglican Communion and in the ecumenical sphere.

Monday **Day 27**

HUMAN STANDARDS

I ask that when I am present I need not show boldness by daring to oppose those who think we are acting according to human standards. Indeed, we live as human beings, but we do not wage war according to human standards. (2 Corinthians 10:2–3)

When threatened, our natural reaction is to defend. This can be expressed as silent bitterness, passive aggression, or hostile attack.

When our personal integrity is attacked, the grievance travels with us. Sometimes it is as obvious as having a dog on a lead. At times it is less conspicuous, but equally present.

We tend to respond to insults with the weapons used by our opponents. But we sharpen them with our anger and hurt. If they wound us with innuendo, backbiting, and cutting remarks, should we not, in righteous indignation, do the same? If they campaign with lies, should not we dilute the truth a little? 'Everyone else does it, so why can't I?'

Paul was faced with the dilemma of being human. But boldness would accomplish nothing. We choose not to apply human standards.

Justice defies vengeance. The church and its leaders must respond to issues that touch personal integrity. But our standard of justice is the Cross of Christ, where injustice bought redemption, suffering bred forgiveness, and evil produced eternal reconciliation.

Paul Oestreicher in his book *The double cross* provides a challenging example:

> Windhoek, Pretoria, Berlin, Prague and finally – Auschwitz. I did not really want to go. I had been to enough former concentration camps turned into museums of horror ... A medical student who spoke good English was my guide. It was her holiday job. She did it well, without the usual heavy pathos. And without the anti-fascist slogans. Why waste words here?

Oestreicher describes the feelings that surfaced for him as he remembered his grandmother who had taken her own life, and the relatives and friends who had been gassed to death. In the reception room he is handed a book filled with expressions of bitterness, anger, shame and horror.

I could only, without words, try to pray and then write the timeless words 'Father forgive'. My student guide took one look, shook her head and walked away. Was that not a kind of blasphemy? To forgive that?

Jesus, you spoke with passion,
you acted without fear, and we remember.
Help us when we have to speak out, to speak the truth
and without malice to speak.

DISCUSSION

How are we enslaved by our human standards? How do we find freedom from the slavery of vengeance? How do we find our healing in the gift of the Cross?

LAMBETH 98: Called to be faithful in a plural world

Communion literally means 'holding something in common'. All humanity shares in common the potential to respond to the life of God. The church holds in common that this life is revealed and offered to the world by Jesus Christ. Within the Anglican Communion, this experience of a common life has traditionally been expressed in the doctrinal and structural features of the different provinces. Anglicans are 'in communion' because of their shared understanding of catholic faith and order, their sacramental and liturgical inheritance, and the interlocking history of their churches.

Communion also defines the relationship between humankind and God. On the human level it is love, understood as solidarity ('God has made of one blood all the peoples who dwell on the face of the whole earth [Acts 17:26]) and relationships of respect and justice ('Those who do not love a brother or sister whom they have seen cannot love God whom they have not seen' [1 John 4:20]).

In the words of the World Council of Churches' Commission on Faith and Order *(Towards koinonia in faith, life and witness: Draft of a working document 1992)*, the communion which God intended for humankind is 'a participation in the life of God through [the Word] in the Holy Spirit, a shared life within communion in unity and diversity' which draws us into the mystery of love which is God's very being.

We perceive the reality of God in a number of ways. We meet God through our participation in the creation. God is also revealed in our experience of human relationships. And God encounters us through the structures by which our relationships with others and the rest of creation are ordered and transmitted from generation to generation.

Tuesday **Day 28**

CAPTIVE TO CHRIST

For the weapons of our warfare are not merely human, but they have divine power to destroy strongholds. We destroy arguments and every proud obstacle raised up against the knowledge of God, and we take every thought captive to obey Christ. (2 Corinthians 10:4–5)

The Jesuit Order, when working with people of other faiths, followed the principle that if you lost any argument after passionate engagement, you often won a convert to Christ.

This principle presumed that Christianity, in the end, is more than concept, doctrine or ideals. It is a presence and a person revealed to us. To use the words of Martin Buber, this revelation can only take place when we treat the other person as a person – a 'thou'. If our relationships and exchanges are limited to 'I and it' then the meeting is devoid of mutuality. More tragically, the eternal 'Thou' is excluded from the exchange. When our interactions move into the realm of 'I and thou', the 'divine order' also enters the relationship.

Paul knew that the gospel revealed to him by Jesus exceeds any obstacle, argument or philosophy that could be put in his way. One who is captive to Christ must account for the faith within, but as Paul reminds us, 'do this with gentleness and sensitivity'.

Other faiths have come to Australia from many parts of the world. They raise questions for the church. How are these persons to be viewed? Are they targets for church growth? Minds with whom to debate? Are they materially and spiritually impoverished, requiring our care as charitable projects? Or do they bear Christ, in a form yet to be determined, understood, loved, and respected by us? How will that fit into our belief that Christ is unique and is the only true face of God? However we answer, if our thinking is captive to Christ, we will make a lasting link with those of other faiths, a link that goes beyond words to an encounter that discovers God's Truth revealed in Christ.

Holy God,
source of all truth, light and love,
you make yourself known in every page of the human story.
You have revealed yourself fully in the face of Jesus Christ.
Help us who live in the power of his Spirit
to discover his influence in those who seek you
and yet are unable to name Christ as Lord.
May we work together in humility and love
that the world may be filled with the knowledge of your love
as the waters cover the sea.

DISCUSSION

How do we bear Christ into our meetings with people of other faiths? How do we meet the other as 'thou'? How does Christ call us to live our faith with joy and integrity?

LAMBETH 98: Called to live and proclaim the Good News

Christianity is sometimes said to be a relation more than a religion. Christian holiness is always living in true and creative relation with God and others, in gratitude to God, in justice with the world.

This may give us some perspective on Christian relations with those of other faiths. The Christian believes that there is finally one hope for human beings – to be in Christ, sharing his complete openness to the loving gift of God his Father. Paul in Acts 17 suggests that this hope may be both a fulfilment of human aspirations as people seek after God, and also a judgment on the extent to which those aspirations are misdirected. If God's active life of reaching out in love has truly come into our lives, we shall always be showing to the world who our God is, and what our God is like. In some circumstances it will be hard or impossible to do this in any other way than by faithful endurance, especially where Christians are a powerless or persecuted minority. In other contexts it is possible, indeed necessary, to find ways of keeping the proclamation of the faith clearly in the public view; this may be particularly important in secularised environments. The glory and distinctiveness of the gift we have received in Jesus is visible, attracting and inviting.

Christian faith is a matter of invitation, not force or threat. Christians are truly engaged in mission when they seek to serve those of other faiths, to defend their proper rights and share insights with them, just as much as when they speak directly of God's call. This may involve a special concern for the needs of religious minorities. Abuse or dismissal of other faiths, or any attempt to bully or manipulate others into Christian commitment are distortions of true Christian faithfulness.

Inter-religious conflict is a tragically complex matter. The church has to acknowledge many sinful distortions in its history. We might think of the terrible treatment of Muslims and Christians at each other's hands in Bosnia in recent years. In parts of the world, Christians suffer acutely from the aggression of others who belong to different faiths even though such aggression represents a distorted version of those other faiths. Bishops in such situations need the fullest support and understanding of other churches as they struggle to protect and guide their people.

The problem is always how to balance the joyful confidence of a faith that reaches out with the courtesy, patience, and prudence that equally belong to the lifestyle of those living in Christ. We are right to give thanks that God's love and justice are so often honoured and made manifest in the lives of people of other faiths. This becomes clear in a very distinctive way when Christians find themselves working alongside those of other faiths for the sake of the needy and the excluded. And yet we retain the conviction that this love and justice are the gift of Jesus Christ and find their full meaning in relation to the hope he has brought into the world.

Wednesday **Day 29**

DISCIPLINE

We are ready to punish every disobedience when your obedience is complete. (2 Corinthians 10:6)

Obedience and discipline have become negative concepts in a world where the individual reigns supreme, and where any demand on a person is regarded as stifling the human personality.

Another trend of modern society is to institute laws and ethical guidelines to regulate human relations. Falsely we believe that, if we codify all aspects of human behaviour, we will create a climate of tolerance and mutual respect. We seek to enshrine the higher value of equal dignity and human worth through legislation, requiring tolerance of people of differing gender, age, colour, and creed. However worthy our laws, they cannot meet God's call to obedience.

Paul faced serious matters concerning human relations. For Christians, issues of human sexuality are a source of great conflict. One response is to resolve the debate by asserting sexuality to be a matter of discipline, and obedience to 'God's law'. Some called Paul to take a stern stand and punish those who had created dissension. Paul called the Corinthian church to be 'complete' in its own obedience. Before demanding stern punishment of others for 'disobedience', examine your own focus on Jesus Christ.

In *Come listen live,* a set of Bible studies compiled by the Diocese of Newcastle, people told how God had transformed their views of the world. One moving story was written by a woman whose brother had died of AIDS.

> My baby brother Jon was an outrageously funny man whose audacious wit and animation livened up any gathering.
>
> He died three years ago, aged 27, having gradually deteriorated physically and mentally through AIDS. He had kept his HIV status secret from us, so we had a very short time to do a lot of unfinished emotional business. We began a nightmare journey of pain and self-knowledge that still continues for me, though he at last has found his safe harbour, or so I hope and pray.
>
> When someone you love has AIDS you are confronted with so many issues: sexuality, love, fear of infection, fear of death, what to tell the children, how to share a meal together. I learned how people who are gay feel so enormously rejected and unacceptable in our society and especially by people who go to church. I learned how hard it is to give unconditional love and what enormous power it has to heal our hearts.

Eternal God,
you call us to a life of holy obedience
to you and to your way set forth in Jesus:
you do not abandon us when we fail to obey or to follow;
help us not to abandon those whom we judge to be sinful:
Give us the humility to offer all of life to you
and to cast ourselves on your mercy –
for you alone can save.

DISCUSSION

What does 'obedience' mean in the Christian journey? What are the marks of an obedient Christian community?

LAMBETH 98: Called to full humanity

In family and sexual relations the moral challenge of globalisation is evident.

With a rapid decline in two-parent families in many parts of the world, a rise in both teenage pregnancies and abortions, increasing evidence about child abuse and violence against women, and widespread confusion about the legal and social limits of pornography and obscenity, church leaders are currently facing an enormous challenge to what has often been regarded as their traditional teaching.

Two key biblical virtues that are held in tension on the issue of sexuality are crucial as we seek to live in a more Christ-like way – loving kindness and faithfulness on the one hand and righteousness and justice on the other. God's loving kindness in the Old Testament is continued in the New Testament in the form of love and grace.

A doctrine of the atonement allows us to set these two ways of seeing God's relationship to the world into a context of our relationships to each other as human beings. Just as God has related to us, so we should try to relate to each other: each of us is called to live a faithful and Christ-like life, not least in an area of such vulnerability as our human sexuality.

An abiding pattern is faithful and loving monogamy, which is seen as the Christian way for both sexual relationships in general and for the responsible bringing up of children. Nevertheless, customary marriage and polygamy are seen as less than ideal but not as inherently opposed to this ideal.

Inter-cultural readings of the Bible have helped to show how we change, our context changes and our perception of the Bible changes. If this had not been the case then Christianity would soon have become moribund and anachronistic. Nevertheless, we are spared from pure relativism, becoming in the process little more than echoes of our surrounding societies, by our constant interactions with Christian texts especially in a context of Christian worship.

Thursday **Day 30**

BELONGING TO CHRIST

Look at what is before your eyes. If you are confident that you belong to Christ, remind yourself of this, that just as you belong to Christ, so also do we. (2 Corinthians 10:7)

A former Head of State in Sri Lanka, a staunch Buddhist, used to ridicule the Christian churches with the jibe, 'Every one of you says that you are the only one, true, authentic church and that all the others are cheap imitations. In none can a Buddhist find the greatest virtue of all, mutual compassion.'

Last year a group of Christians in New South Wales wrote to their local church seeking funds to establish a mission in an area where they asserted there were only three Bible-believing, Christ-centred churches. Yet that area had over 50 churches of various traditions!

Paul faced a test of his orthodoxy. A group in Corinth asserted that they alone belonged to Christ. They believed Paul had received a half-baked revelation and preached an unorthodox gospel. Paul invites the Corinthians to look at the evidence before them. Christ is preached but Christ-like behaviour is lacking.

No one owns Christ. Christ does the choosing. The choice becomes evident in how Christians relate to each other and to the world around them.

'Look at what is before your eyes.' The evidence is what matters. Christlikeness – portrayed in the life of the individual and the church – speaks more than words believed and doctrines taught.

Christianity has provided the world with great saints and supreme acts of altruism. Still the Inquisition, witch hunts, bigotry and hatred cannot be erased from the memory of the world. We must recall both aspects of our history, and remain humble and vigilant.

Holy One, holy and eternal,
awesome, exciting and delightful in your holiness;
make us pure in heart to see you;
make us merciful to receive your kindness
and to share our love with all your human family;
then will your name be hallowed on earth as in heaven.

DISCUSSION

How do we as a local church find unity with others? How do we tell the story of Christ in ways that draw us together?

LAMBETH 98: Called to be one

The church is given the task of preaching 'at-one-ment'. We may grow weary of attempting to surmount the deeply entrenched obstacles which divide Christians from one another. We may fear the risk involved in the messiness of moving to greater visible unity. Yet we rejoice that significant progress has been made since Lambeth 1988. We are not excused from the task of loving one another, and of seeking to embody 'at-one-ment' in the life of the church, because of the greatness of the love with which God has loved us, and the extreme cost of the forgiveness of our sins. The unforgettable price of the fellowship we have with God, and therefore with one another, consists in the fact that 'the blood of Jesus Christ cleanses us from all sin' (1 John 1:7).

Lambeth Conferences have always been concerned with the unity of the church. From 1878 they have drawn inspiration from the great intercessory prayer in which our Lord pleaded for the unity of his church, coupling it with intercessions for the enlargement of his kingdom. From 1888 resolutions have concerned relations with other churches. In 1998, therefore, we seek further inspiration from the one and only source of all fellowship, and open ourselves in heart and mind to God's call to us to preach and to embody 'at-one-ment' in new ways.

First we need rigorously to test our historical commitment to the goal of visible unity against an understanding of legitimate diversity, what we are experiencing already as Christians, and the current direction of the ecumenical dialogues. Secondly, we have to assess the progress that has been made in our present dialogues, both bilateral and multilateral. Finally, we have to consider the pastoral and ecumenical issues arising out of Anglican experience of new churches and independent Christian groups. In each theme we need to consider how the encounter with people of other faiths generates a new set of relationships and ask how these relate to our ecumenical vocation. More practically, Christians are often asked to join people of other faiths in common celebrations or remembrances, and action for justice, peace and the care of creation.

Called to be faithful in a plural world

The faith we share not only looks back to its origins; it also points forward to the time when God will be all in all. Meanwhile, the church has the responsibility to ground its hopes and incarnate its faith in the diverse realities of its own generation.

Friday ***Day 31***

LETTERS

Now, even if I boast a little too much of our authority, which the Lord gave for building you up and not for tearing you down, I will not be ashamed of it. I do not want to seem as though I am trying to frighten you with my letters. For they say, 'His letters are weighty and strong, but his bodily presence is weak, and his speech contemptible.' Let such people understand that what we say by letter when absent, we will also do when present. (2 Corinthians 10:8–11)

Letters are a vital part of our communication one with another. Even in this age of e-mail, faxes and the ability to have instant verbal communication over vast distances, a letter has an impact.

Precious to me is a letter I received during a retreat in preparation for my ordination as a deacon. It was from a priest who had visited our home and dragged me off for confirmation classes. He was in his seventies, wore a black cassock, cape and skull cap, and was known as Dracula. Later, I was called back to Christ after a teenage sojourn outside church structures. At my ordination retreat I read:

> Dear Roger, you rascal. The Hound of Heaven has finally caught up with you. I hope it continues to bite you! From the day of your confirmation I have prayed for you. Yours affectionately, Fr Charlie (Dracula).

This letter gave me an overwhelming sense of the power of prayer and of the silent care that sustains me.

We are grateful today for some of the 'goings-on' in Corinth, as well as for some of the opponents to Paul. Through them we meet and know a person close to Christ and close to the world of that infant Christian community.

The Holy Scriptures, like 'letters', are a beautiful communication system. The Holy Spirit enables the interaction between the writers, a particular context, the present world and the ever-present Word of God. The letters we write will never make the Canon of Holy Writ. They can, however, make all the difference in someone's life!

Bountiful God, we thank you for planting in us
the seed of your word:
by your Holy Spirit, help us to receive it with joy
and to live according to it,
that we may grow in faith and hope and love.

DISCUSSION

What letters have been precious for you? Are there times when Holy Scripture has brought a precious message for you?

LAMBETH 98: Called to live and proclaim the Good News

Scripture is a place where we expect to encounter a God who calls. In the community of those called to walk with Jesus, the call is constantly renewed by exposure to the Bible. Churches that are really on the move throughout the world are listening gratefully and joyfully to Scripture. Here the voice of God, made real in the history of Israel and the life of Jesus and the witness of the early communities of believers, becomes immediate to us. We discover afresh that we are already objects of God's mission even before we know we are agents. We remember that God's mission has been on its way to us since before the world was made. Mission demands faithfulness to the Bible as a living challenge, and as a promise of transformation.

Called to be faithful in a plural world

Paul and the other New Testament writers sought to understand and express the gospel in the terms of their times and culture, and Christians continue to do the same today. In our highly plural context that challenge is especially acute.

As Lambeth Conference 1988 states, 'Anglicans are held together by the characteristic way in which they use Scripture, tradition and reason in discerning afresh the mind of Christ for the church in each generation.' We also recognise that such discernment would always arise from the life of prayer and attention to the experience of other Christians.

Scripture remains as the 'rule and ultimate standard' (Chicago-Lambeth Quadrilateral, Lambeth Conference 1888, Resolution 11 (A)) of Christian faith, yet the Scripture writers were themselves faced with the same challenge as we are in seeking to express the gospel faithfully in their particular circumstances. At his incarnation God came to dwell among us, taking our flesh and living in a specific place and time. So, God continues to speak his Word to a given people in a given context.

Saturday ***Day 32***

COMPARISONS

We do not dare to classify or compare ourselves with some of those who commend themselves. But when they measure themselves by one another, and compare themselves with one another, they do not show good sense. (2 Corinthians 10:12)

In the fable Snow White and the Seven Dwarfs, the jealous stepmother stands before the mirror with the question that made her a cold-blooded murderer: 'Mirror, mirror on the wall, who is the fairest of us all?'

Over history, churches have looked at the mirror of self-interest and asked, 'Who is the fairest of us all? Roman Catholic, Anglican, Orthodox, Presbyterian, Baptist, Uniting?'

In the last few decades over 600 new churches have formed, most of them from the United States. Each offers a different gospel beat; each is caught up with the 'gospel supermarket'. Traditional churches, often described as 'dull, boring and irrelevant', have faced massive decline in numbers. Some have decided to use the gimmicks of the market place; others retreat into being Old World museum pieces. Some stand confused between the crass mediocrity of the gospel sales pitch arena and the world of beauty and grandeur of language and music in 'old-time religion'.

Richard Holloway in his book *The stranger in the wings* observes that the Anglican Church is particularly well-placed to respond to the discomfort caused by pluralism:

> For many years we have been a pluralist culture in our own right, and discord is part of our way of life. In fact, this is something that has characterised Christianity from the beginning ... Truth-seeking involves us inescapably in conflict ... When human beings search for truth, they come up against the phenomenon of truths that are in opposition to each other. Most of the conflicts that characterise human history are not about the battle between right and wrong, truth and error, but the battle between opposing rights or opposing truths.

Paul dealt with the crisis of comparisons using the mirror of Christ as judge. Faced with that revelation, comparison and commendation become repugnant.

Eternal and glorious God,
you dwell in a high and holy place,
yet draw us near in your beloved Son;
we humble ourselves before you and pray that we may know
your loving presence.

DISCUSSION

How does the local church address the tension of maintaining tradition and preaching the gospel in the 20th century? Do we know and share the deep meaning of our tradition? Are we open to new ways of sharing Christ's message of salvation with the world?

LAMBETH 98: Called to be one

When the agenda for the Lambeth Conference was being formulated, the responses from the regions indicated that there was a difficulty in almost every part of the Anglican Communion in establishing good and constructive relations with Pentecostal and fundamentalist churches.

> **West Indies:** The growth of Pentecostalism in the area influences issues regarding baptism and charismatic renewal. Fundamentalism (often imported from northern media), is an issue: Scripture is often used to support ideologies.

Southern Africa: Fundamentalism which is narrow, divisive, exclusive and unaccommodating, is a major threat to unity. The state of transition through which Southern Africa is going results in feelings of deep insecurity on the part of many who then seek the certainty offered by fundamentalist faiths. This retreat into fundamentalism is in itself a threat to unity and peace, and is a destabilising factor. The fundamentalist churches challenge the church of the Province of Southern Africa, however, offering as they do an enthusiasm, a measure of community support, and a degree of biblical teaching not often found in Anglican churches.

West Africa: This topic ... has a particular West African manifestation in the rise of the charismatic movement and the proliferation of African Independent and Sectarian churches. What is the Anglican response as regards (a) ecumenism and (b) church order?

East Asia: Concern was expressed over the development of the work and mission of mainly American fundamentalist churches. They operated very independently and gave a bad image to the rest of the world.

Indian Ocean: The fundamentalist movements tend to emphasise the differences between themselves and ourselves, rather than reaching towards ecumenism. Because of their lively interpretation of the Bible, they tend to be attractive to younger people and are thus seen to be a threat to the Anglican Church and other established churches, and also to ecumenism.

West Asia and the Middle East: We noted the presence of fundamentalist churches and para-church organisations in our region and their often damaging impact. In relation to them we need to ask what we mean by Christian fundamentalism and to determine criteria for engaging in dialogue and co-operation with them. The criteria we would recommend are: Trinitarian belief; mutual recognition of baptism; affirmation of the two natures of Christ.

It is generally acknowledged by the churches in Western cultures that fundamentalist and Pentecostal churches and groups play a significant and growing part in religious and public life.

Sunday ***Day 33***

FOOLISHNESS

I wish you would bear with me in a little foolishness. Do bear with me! I feel a divine jealousy for you, for I promised you in marriage to one husband, to present you as a chaste virgin to Christ.
(2 Corinthians 11:1–2)

In the East, a significant person in the village is the matchmaker. Dressed in white with a black umbrella under his left arm he travels from one part of the community to the other making links. His reputation stands or falls on his powers of observation, on historical knowledge of the families involved and on reading personalities.

In Genesis 24, Abraham's servant tested his choice of a future wife for Isaac with her propensity to be hospitable, not only to him, but to the camels as well! Because women were seen as a part of property transactions and as bearers of children for male inheritance, virginity and chasteness became a vital part of the transaction. The duty of the matchmaker is to see, not only that the property transactions are uncompromised, but that the woman to be married is 'pure'.

Paul saw himself in the role of matchmaker, presenting to Christ a church uncompromised and pure. Paul's concepts of womanhood were influenced by his strict rabbinical upbringing. In the Aramaic world, purity was a consistency in loving endeavour as powerful as a bud blossoming into a flower. Its roots were linked to electrifying flashes of lightning offering a vision of sheer, dazzling beauty and power. Purity was not limited to gender, for it belonged to God's very nature. Those washed in the waters of baptism were to have the quality of loving endeavour that maintains the church as a true partner to Christ in God's world.

There is a story told of a now extinct monkey kingdom. As part of puberty rites, a young monkey was given a stick. At a given signal, each was to strike everything in its path, subdue it, and kill it if it resisted. Those who competed with the greatest ferocity achieved adulthood. A further aspect of the ritual was more bizarre. Any monkey, male or female, that aided those who had been subdued or wounded was declared an outcast. Outcasts were hung by their legs from the upper branches of the trees to die the painful death of cowards and be eaten by vultures and vermin.

Today there is no monkey kingdom, no males or females, no heroes or cowards, no strong or weak.

All that remains are the trees. On a still night, you can hear the branches whisper to one another, 'Compassion. Is it for fools? Purity. Has it been lost? Will no-one grieve for them any more?'

Blessed are you, O God;
you call your church to share your vibrant life of purity.
Dare us by your compassion
to be foolish in our witness and service for you;
that the world may discover you as its only true lover
and faithful friend.

DISCUSSION

How do we in the local community live into the purity and holiness of our baptismal calling? How do we mimic the world's values of power and might? How do we offer compassion to people who are neglected and battered? Do we grieve for the unloved in our world?

LAMBETH 98: Called to be one

The Scriptures offer us a portrait of a church living wholeheartedly in the light of the gospel:

- it is a church rooted and grounded in the love and grace of the Lord Christ;
- it is a church always joyful, praying continually and giving thanks even in the midst of suffering;
- it is a pilgrim church, a people of God with a new heavenly citizenship, a holy nation and a royal priesthood;
- it is a church which makes common confession of the apostolic faith in word and in life, the faith common to the whole church everywhere and at all times;
- it is a church with a mission to all in every race and nation, preaching the gospel, proclaiming the forgiveness of sins, baptising and celebrating the Eucharist;
- it is a church which is served by an ordained apostolic ministry, sent by God to gather and nourish the people of God in each place, uniting and linking them with the church universal within the whole communion of saints;
- it is a church which manifests through its visible communion the healing and uniting power of God amidst the divisions of humankind;

- it is a church in which the bonds of communion are strong enough to enable it to bear effective witness in the world, to guard and interpret the apostolic faith, to take decisions, to teach authoritatively, and to share its goods with those in need;
- it is a church alive and responsive to the hope which God has set before it, to the wealth and glory of the share God has offered it in the heritage of his people, and to the vastness of the resources of God's power open to those who trust in him.

(from *The Porvoo Common Statement, Together in Mission and Ministry* (1993))

Such a portrait enables us to see ways in which the life of our own church is challenged to repentance and transformation; and also to recognise in the life of fellow Christians in other churches a true participation in the apostolic faith and mission of the whole people of God.

Monday **Day 34**

DECEPTION

But I am afraid that as the serpent deceived Eve by its cunning, your thoughts will be led astray from a sincere and pure devotion to Christ. For if someone comes and proclaims another Jesus than the one we proclaimed, or if you receive a different spirit from the one you received, or a different gospel from the one you accepted, you submit to it readily enough. (2 Corinthians 11:3–4)

The garden of Eden has a great deal to answer for! Bishop Yong Ping Chung, Bishop of Sabah, suggested that Adam and Eve were actually Australians from Tasmania, hence the preoccupation with apples. 'If they had been Chinese,' he said, 'they would have ignored the apple and eaten the snake!' Unfortunately the biblical narrative, a poetic musing on our beginnings, has been used by some people to provide a framework for ordering human relationships that has done damage to women in every age. Paul turned to the story of Eve, one who was deceived, to exemplify the fickleness of the Corinthians. Like Eve, they were being deceived by those seeking to undermine Paul's ministry.

Recent Hebrew scholarship has challenged the hierarchy of roles to provide an alternative view of the ancient burden of guilt and deceit women have had to bear because of the Genesis narrative. In *God and the rhetoric of sexuality,* Phyllis Trible writes:

> The response of the woman to the serpent reveals her as intelligent, informed, and perceptive ... Her words of uncompromising obedience are at the centre of scene two. Yet the centre cannot hold ...
> The expansion of life at the beginning of the story disintegrates at its end ... Joy in the garden dissipates in the sorrow of exile, with disobedience as the turning point ... The divine, human, animal, and plant worlds are all adversely affected ... Estranged from each other, the man and the woman are banished from the garden and barred forever from the tree of life. Truly, a love story has gone awry.
> Yet Genesis 2–3 is not the only word in Scripture on human sexuality. What it forfeits in tragedy, the Song of Songs redeems in joy.

The Song of Jesus, the Spirit of Jesus, the gospel of Jesus, says Paul, must stand the test of all deceit. It must give way to an obedience that is mutual and life-giving.

Eternal Word of God,
we acknowledge the alienation we bring upon ourselves
by ignoring your voice,
and listening instead to the serpents within and around us.
Forgive us for the blame, shame, prejudice and hate we have
caused to all the 'daughters of Eve'.
Grant us a new beginning, in Christ, that celebrates the differences
between women and men and unites us in listening attentively to
your Word that brings true oneness and life to all.

DISCUSSION

A question still remains for our times:

Have we in the name of power, domination and subjugation preached another Jesus to our world? How do different cultural understandings of family and other relationships affect life in your church?

LAMBETH 98: Called to be faithful in a plural world

The New Testament testifies to the fact that Christian faith should affect the way faithful people live their lives. Paul and others identify a number of ethical standards for the sake of the Christian community. While the principles expressed in these ethical standards remain the same, they may be understood differently in different cultures and contexts. This can be illustrated by the variety of approaches to issues of money, marriage, family and sexual relations.

Behind the differences in how family members are appropriately related to each other are diverse cultural assumptions about how human beings live together. Degrees of physical intimacy, different assumptions about individualism, the role of women in society, relationships between members of the same and the opposite sex, kinship patterns, behaviour between parents and children, and the problems of overpopulation are only a few of the most obvious issues that divide people across the spectrum of cultural diversity. All of these questions must be submitted to the ethical teaching of the New Testament, and fidelity to the gospel.

Tuesday ***Day 35***

SUPER APOSTLE

I think that I am not in the least inferior to these super-apostles. I may be untrained in speech, but not in knowledge; certainly in every way and in all things we have made this evident to you. (2 Corinthians 11:5–6)

Paul was mad – mad with a foolishness born out of jealousy for those he loved in Corinth, mad with a fierce commitment to the truth he had experienced in Jesus, mad with a burning desire to win back those who had been deceived. With a twist of irony and sarcasm, Paul coined a phrase to describe his opponents: 'super-apostles'. Irony in the Greek world was an attractive form of rhetoric providing it was conversational rather than confrontational.

Dr M. M. Thomas, Indian philosopher and theologian, used to warn his students, 'Watch out for that which is most creative in you, guard it and nurture it passionately, but remember, where the creation is, there is the fall.' Your greatest gifts can be your greatest source of temptation, the place where you are the most vulnerable.

Christian ministry is always dangerous. Eloquence in preaching, studious knowledge of Scripture, the drama of presiding in the liturgy in colourful, embroidered vestments, responding to those in need of prayerful pastoral concern, chairing the local parish council: our very service for others can become a self-indulgent exercise. It can lead us, like Paul, into anger and into characterising our opponents with cheaply-coined and damaging phrases. It can lead us to protect our role rather than those we are called to serve.

A 1992 survey found the church had created a world of super-apostles, the ordained, and a world of inferior apostles, the people. We need to rediscover the true nature of the people called by God. The church is the people. The authority of Holy Orders is derived from the baptised community to enable all to live out their baptismal covenants.

In an ancient jungle prone to fires lived a tribe of monkeys. They selected a leader: big, wise, strong and able. One day a great fire broke out in the jungle. The leader swiftly moved the tribe to the stream at the edge of the forest. Its gentle flow had become a torrent of water, for the snow on the mountains was melting. The tribe was trapped, with the fire rushing relentlessly towards them. The leader stretched across the raging water, two front paws gripping one bank, the back paws clinging to the other. The tribe began to move across this living bridge. When the oldest had hobbled across the living bridge to reach the other side the raging fire reduced the body of the leader to ashes.

Ever since then the tribe have returned to the river to drink from the stream and to remind themselves what true leadership is about.

**Everlasting God, your Son Jesus Christ girded himself with a towel and washed his disciples' feet;
grant us the will to be the servant of others as he was servant of all,
who gave up his life and died for us, yet lives and reigns with you
and the Holy Spirit, one God now and for ever.**

DISCUSSION

How are all people in our local parish being supported in their baptismal calling? Where do we find examples of sacrificial leadership?

LAMBETH 98: Called to be faithful in a plural world

Baptism into Christ is the foundation of all Christian ministry. Through baptism, each follower of Christ is called into that ministry and given the gifts necessary to carry it out. Paul's celebration of the variety of the Spirit's gifts and their usefulness in accomplishing God's purposes (1 Corinthians 12:8–10) is echoed in the WCC document *Baptism, Eucharist and Ministry* (1982):

> All members are called to discover, with the help of the community, the gifts they have received, and to use them for the building up of the church and for the service of the world to which the church is sent.

The baptised and empowered community is a Eucharist community, receiving ongoing strengthening and nourishment for mission and ministry, by being fed with the body and blood, the very life, of its self-giving and risen Lord.

The church is most faithful to its calling when all its members are aware of their vocation as disciples of Christ, and that they received that vocation in their baptism, whatever their ministry. This awareness is strengthened in a number of Provinces of the Anglican Communion through emphasis on the promises made in baptism. While the specific words differ from Province to Province, baptismal promises highlight five commitments directly related to the ministry of the people as body of Christ, none of which is more important than the others. These are worship, proclamation or evangelisation, forgiveness or reconciliation, service and working for justice.

It is always a distortion when some ministries are exercised in such a way as to diminish the full significance of others. This is particularly a danger for the ordained ministry, called to build up the ministry of all the members of Christ's Body through preaching, teaching and sacramental ministry.

In one Province's Episcopal ordination service candidates are asked: 'Will you encourage and support all baptised people in their gifts and ministries?' As a leader and on behalf of the whole church, the bishop responds: 'I will.'

A lay theologian has recently written:

> While the reason for seeing the clergy as the 'continuum' of the church is understandable, the truth is [that] this has led to a widespread perception by the laity themselves as 'second class' spiritually: and sadly some clergy give the strong impression that they support this view. (Dr Ruth Etchells, 'Reflections on Lay Ministry,' 1997, p5)

Wednesday **Day 36**

PRESSURE OF CHURCHES

And, besides other things, I am under daily pressure because of my anxiety for all the churches. Who is weak, and I am not weak? Who is made to stumble, and I am not indignant? If I must boast, I will boast of the things that show my weakness. The God and Father of the Lord Jesus (blessed be he forever!) knows that I do not lie. In Damascus, the governor under King Aretas guarded the city of Damascus in order to seize me, but I was let down in a basket through a window in the wall, and escaped from his hands. (2 Corinthians 11:28–33)

Paul's meeting with Christ on the road to Damascus had brought him enemies, hardship, and tribulation. A litany of woes! 'No,' he says, 'for God has given me a new way of looking at life. It is an upside down view!'

With change can come scandal and rejection, or joy in knowing one's life is hidden in Christ. Both scandal and joy are contained within the fellowship of the gospel. This view was different to what Paul had been taught as a strict Pharisee – the righteous are placed above humiliation. It was at variance with the culture of the Middle East with its clear distinction between honour and shame. It ran counter to Greek philosophy that idealised the hero and ridiculed the weak. Paul had already challenged this view in 1 Corinthians: the foolishness of God is wiser than human wisdom; God's weakness is stronger than human strength. The crucified Christ, humiliated, weak and foolish, is at the centre of God's act of salvation. Paul reminds the Corinthians that in Damascus he was forced to take the coward's exit. Ben Witherington III says in *Conflict and community in Corinth:*

> In Acts the story is told as an example of Paul's and the early Christians' courage and cleverness; here he uses it as a sign of his weakness, boasting of what happens to him rather than of what he is able to accomplish.
>
> One of the keys to understanding why Paul includes this apparently anti heroic tale is the Roman military honour called the *corona muralis,* the 'wall crown'. This was one of the highest military awards and was given to the soldier who was first to scale the wall into an enemy city ... Paul is saying that while the typical Roman hero is first up the wall, he is first down the wall!

What a common experience of the evangelist, the pastor, the leader or the church! When we think that we have failed utterly, when we are rendered most vulnerable, there we have been most effective. To travel into the whirlwind requires a new sense of vulnerability and a deep level of trust.

Giver of the present, hope for the future:
save us from the time of trial.
When prophets warn us of doom, of catastrophe
and of suffering beyond belief
then, God, free us from our helplessness, and deliver us from evil.
Save us from our arrogance and folly, for you are God who created the world; you have redeemed us and you are our salvation.

DISCUSSION

How have we known risk and vulnerability? How has God turned our weakness upside down? How have we found strength in danger, salvation in loss, pride in humiliation? Where is Christ in all this?

LAMBETH 98: Called to live and proclaim the Good News

The more we let divine action through, in our plans, words and acts, the more it will achieve its purpose. God's Word does not return empty but accomplishes its purpose. Hence we can say, with Paul, that the One who calls is faithful, and that the One who calls equips us with what we need. We can rely on the promise of Jesus as he sends his followers on his business, that he will be with them always.

The trouble is, of course, that we so readily turn to forms and structures and attitudes that seem to get in the way of the divine act of mission. But it may still help to remember that Jesus didn't say, 'I am with you when you're doing well', but 'I am with you always.' He is with us when we blunder and fail; and sometimes the most effective release of mission comes when we face our failures. Our honest repentance can give more room to God than a success that is feeding our self-satisfaction.

To be a minister in Christ's church, especially one called to the leadership and responsibility of a bishop, is to be entrusted with renewing the sense of being called, and endowed and sent by God among all God's people. The bishop is both an agent and an inspirer of mission. In the early church, the bishop instructed and initiated all new Christians and expounded Scripture to them daily. Modern conditions make this rather harder! But the bishop must still be, above all, someone who works to present the call of God to the whole church as vividly as possible. If there is a justification for the way our ministry is structured, it must be in terms of how those structures serve mission – how they help that process by which the call of God becomes concrete and compelling.

And this points up the need for bishops to know that *they,* along with all God's people, are receivers of mission and bearers of Good News. The structures of the Anglican Communion, from parish to diocese to the Lambeth Conference, must be judged by how far they assist God's people to hear and answer God's call.

Thursday **Day 37**

VISIONS AND REVELATIONS

It is necessary to boast; nothing is to be gained by it, but I will go on to visions and revelations of the Lord. I know a person in Christ who fourteen years ago was caught up to the third heaven – whether in the body or out of the body I do not know; God knows. (2 Corinthians 12:1–2)

Many in our world are fascinated by any unusual experience. The great Hollywood movie machine has cashed in on the 'other' dimension. Fascination with a world beyond our perception has created an interest in 'psychic' gurus.

The smorgasbord of religious ideas in the New Age movement reflects a yearning to go beyond computer technology. Cyberspace mechanics, however sophisticated, cannot move us into a transcendent reality. Drug and alcohol abuse has reached epic proportions in the western world, another indicator of the desire to 'go beyond'. Could Augustine have been right, 'You have made us for yourself and our hearts are restless until they find their rest in you'?

Religions and religious people who can speak of out-of-the-body experiences can be sure of a following. Paul found this to be true in the world in Corinth. His experience on the road to Damascus had put him directly in touch with the risen Jesus. The writer of Acts had Paul describe this event three times. Still, when Paul wrote about it himself we find a certain reticence. He seems to feel the power of this holy encounter would be lost in the telling. In response to those who claimed a superior mystical experience, Paul spoke reluctantly of his moment of revelation. If it was used to gain extra marks, it would yield nothing. It was a 'holy moment' that demanded painful change.

The event was significant for Paul because it was not of his doing – it was beyond his power. He had been caught up by God in Christ, and Jesus had never let him go. The vision and revelation is ultimately measured not by the hype that accompanies it but by faithfulness.

God of all delight,
grant us that joy which none can take from us,
of having a work to do, a life to live;
that joy in believing which will carry us through temptation,
anxiety and grief.

DISCUSSION

How is my faith more than a feel-good experience? How do the noise and chemicals and technologies of our culture draw us from the experience of Christ? How have I known Christ in my life?

LAMBETH 98: Called to be one

The largest element in Pentecostal groups focuses on the gifts of the Holy Spirit. Some have (or had) a North American component but now mostly possess indigenous roots, sometimes of long standing. They are usually spread by nationals and are both financially and organisationally independent, and prone to splitting. They are found in the Caribbean, Latin America, Africa South of the Sahara and Eastern Europe, as well as in India, China and the Pacific rim. Their spread has more to do with global communications and social and geographical mobility than conventional missionary work. They are an aspect of the multiculturalism of the modern world, and represent the principle of market competition in religion. For this reason, if for no other, traditional churches are irritated and challenged by their activities.

Where they meet with 'native' religions they sometimes incorporate major 'native' elements, sometimes vigorously reject them. The recent emphasis on health and wealth fits in particularly well with the universal search for bodily, moral and material goods. So far as classical Pentecostalism is concerned, health and wealth is a subordinate theme, related to healing miracles, exorcism and the fruits of the economic spirit, and there is little by way of a promise of prosperity. In neo-Pentecostalism, however, prosperity has become a major theme, sometimes drawing on the teaching of parts of the Old Testament, sometimes upon promises of enrichment of a barely disguised commercial character. This latter strain of Pentecostalism is not dominant, but it is increasing its influence, especially in middle class contexts. Moreover, the older Pentecostalism and even the mainstream churches are pushed to incorporate similar elements in their theological understanding. North American influence is most likely in countries such as Liberia, South Korea and the Philippines. Some of these new churches and movements have now themselves begun to engage in missionary activity in other countries.

Friday ***Day 38***

GOD KNOWS

And I know that such a person – whether in the body or out of the body I do not know; God knows – was caught up into Paradise and heard things that are not to be told, that no mortal is permitted to repeat. (2 Corinthians 12:3–4)

In common parlance, the phrase 'God knows' is an expression of ignorance on a subject. For Paul it was a religious affirmation. The dissenters in Corinth were focusing on the ecstatic and the unusual. They suggested Paul did not have these particular gifts. Even if he did, he chose not to describe them in detail. Paul instead pointed to an encounter with God that went beyond human communication and was not a cause for celebrity. The Christian community might be caught up, if God willed it, in ecstatic experiences. But the test of that experience was in how they carried that experience into daily living.

Living in the moment of conversion was not how Paul saw 'calling out' and 'sending out'. God knows, we need those moments when we are lifted up into a Presence that takes our breath and words away. God knows, we need to live our lives daily in the attractiveness of Jesus' grace.

God knows, we need our prayer life lifted from the dutiful to the joyful; our Bible readings and study to become occasions of refreshment; our witness for the gospel to have an easy calmness and a winsome charm. Yes, God knows, we would like to be able to say 'The writing's on the wall, it is the hand of God'. Most often we have to live with the whispers. God knows that is best for us.

Father, imprint upon our hearts
that because we belong to you
no one can pluck us from your hand,
and because we fear you we need fear no other.

DISCUSSION

How does God speak to us in the simple events of life? How does God touch us in the places of amazement and ecstasy? How do these two experiences meet in our own lives?

LAMBETH 98: Called to full humanity

As Christians, we hold in tension a realism about human limitations and hope in the power of transcending love. Thus, the suggestions that follow are both a challenge and an invitation.

In the church:

- The church as a Model Community: A Christian community should be a model of tolerance and love: 'See how they love one another.' Whenever Christians gather they should examine their lifestyle critically and seek to develop honest and affirming relations with one another. The church is the Body of Christ. Encourage participation by all and acknowledge distinctive gifts, cultures and other qualities. The church should identify discriminatory practices in its structures, images and symbols.
- The church as a Moral Community: The Christian community should lay the foundations for moral values that mark a truly human community. Efforts should be made to avoid too close an identification with particular tribal, ethnic or national consciousness. Renewed attention must be paid to the family so as to create an environment where children can be loved and nurtured, especially in this age of widespread social breakdown. Children should be protected from conscription in war and unjust employment practices, and special measures should be taken to meet the needs of unaccompanied child refugees.
- The church as a Learning Community: The church should be open to discover new insights, and to grow in faith and holy living. The church will be devoted to nurturing the faith of children and youth and to receiving those who wish to join the community. The church should teach the elements of Christian formation and promote sensitivity to diverse cultures. Church teaching and community life should reinforce the principle that children need to be protected from the ravages of family violence. Furthermore, it is imperative that the church should do its best to ensure that formal schooling for children is provided in accordance with the International Convention on the Rights of the Child.

In the world:

- In obedience to the teachings of Christ, the church is obliged to promote and protect human rights. The church has a responsibility also to monitor the activities of government and to contribute to the promotion of a just society. The church is called to prophetic witness where human rights violations occur and where corruption and nepotism threaten public trust.
- The church has a role to play in the formation and maintenance of global and local public policy by offering analysis, promoting understanding of public issues, making specific policy proposals and, where necessary and possible, criticising public practice.
- As advocates for peace, the church should encourage the establishment of peace-making agencies to promote conciliation and justice.
- Advocacy on the rights of children should be an important mark of the church in our times.

Saturday ***Day 39***

SPEAKING THE TRUTH

On behalf of such a one I will boast, but on my own behalf I will not boast, except of my weaknesses. But if I wish to boast, I will not be a fool, for I will be speaking the truth. But I refrain from it, so that no one may think better of me than what is seen in me or heard from me, even considering the exceptional character of the revelations.
(2 Corinthians 12:5–7a)

One of the bishops of the Arctic tells the story of a man who had a religious experience and wanted baptism by immersion. God had particularly told him that to receive a full blessing he should be baptised in the river. It was winter, and most rivers were frozen over, but the man insisted on following the divine command. On reaching the spot in the river, a hole was carved out in the ice and the man was duly immersed, with the Trinitarian formula proclaimed by the bishop in tremulous tones – icicles forming on his beard.

The man came out of the water blue and shivering, crying out, 'The Lord be praised. I do not feel the cold.' The bishop's charity had reached fraying point. He said to the deacons, 'Put him back into the water and keep him there until the Spirit of Truth enters his new life in Christ.'

The focus on religious experience alone, be it charismatic, evangelical, catholic or any other, will not benefit the individual Christian or the body of Christ, especially if the 'boast' is seen as an achievement. A claim to religious experience will lack integrity if it has no commitment to truth.

In the case of the super-apostles, their boasting of ecstatic experiences had made them speak lies about Paul.

Paul was at pains to point out that living on emotional or religious highs was of no consequence, even if the revelations were of an exceptional character.

What was required was an infilling of the Spirit of Jesus. Christ who alone is 'all Truth', discerns the truth or falsehood of the experience.

A story is told of a visitor to a monastery who came looking for the purpose and meaning of life. The teacher in the monastery said to the visitor, 'If you've come seeking truth, there is one thing you must have above all else.' 'I know,' said the visitor, 'to find truth you must have an overwhelming passion for it.' 'No,' replied the teacher. 'In order to find truth you must have an unremitting readiness to admit you may be wrong.'

To commit my life to Christ requires a willingness to have the mystic experience tested and the strongly-held belief system scrutinised by the fire of God's Holy Spirit.

Praise to you, God, for all your work among us.
Yours is the vigour in creation,
yours is the impulse in our new discoveries.
Make us adventurous, yet reverent and hopeful in all we do.

DISCUSSION

How does your experience of God in Christ bring you to discover the truth about yourself? How can we test our experience of Jesus and the experiences of others so that boasting does not erase Truth?

LAMBETH 98: Called to be one

Pentecostalism is a movement prone to splitting, adapting to all kinds of social situations, for example, the search for autonomy of young men and women in the tribal cultures of Mexico, or the search for moral reformation and family integration in the university-educated elites of Nigeria. It is led by energetic, semi-educated and male religious entrepreneurs, but it appeals primarily to women as, of course, do the mainstream churches. The appeal to women is that they are offered many opportunities of expression, and gain from a family discipline which reforms the macho male personality.

Worship combines a vigorous assertion of authority and participation. Music is the single most potent element in the appeal of Pentecostal worship, combined with narratives of redemption told in the language of the people.

The most potent element in conversion is the example of lives changed in terms of trust, honest dealing, mutual respect (especially between men and women), mutual support, hard work and disciplined spending in accordance with moral priorities. These virtues, combined with experience in leadership and increased literacy gained in the religious community, lead to modest social mobility. A whole series of questions arise from our diverse experiences of these churches and movements. It is right to ask what we have learned from them about zeal for Christ and the gospel; commitment and giving; community life and mutual support; knowledge of the Scriptures; and joyful and participatory styles of worship.

Critically we may ask about their attitudes towards fellow Christians and the unity of the church; about the adequacy of their interpretation of the Bible on prosperity and suffering; about implicit political or ideological commitments; about styles of leadership; or about the sacraments. In all these matters Anglicans in different parts of the world may have different experiences which are difficult to fit into any coherent shape or pattern. On the other hand they may reflect different stages of development in the church or group concerned, and there may be much to gain from listening to those with stories to tell of the establishment of better relationships in time, or with the rise of a new generation.

Some of the characteristics of the new churches and groups are now to be found inside Anglican churches. Understanding and making positive our own internal diversity is an essential pre-condition for developing good external relationships. The church is called to be a living expression of the gospel, evangelised and evangelising, reconciled and reconciling, gathered together and gathering others. (*Salvation and the Church,* ARCIC, para 28, 1987)

Palm Sunday **Day 40**

THE THORN IN THE FLESH

Therefore, to keep me from being too elated, a thorn was given me in the flesh, a messenger of Satan to torment me, to keep me from being too elated. Three times I appealed to the Lord about this, that it would leave me. (2 Corinthians 12:7b–8)

The problem with Christians who have all the answers is that they do not allow any questions. Human suffering is a strange mystery. The eternal question 'Why?' cries out even in the midst of ardent faith and devotion. We have no easy answers to the question of suffering.

Paul, chosen and set apart to be an apostle to the Gentiles, spoke of his experience in Christ that had taken him into a heavenly realm. Yet he was plagued with a constant gnawing that he described as a 'thorn in the flesh', a 'splinter' that got under his skin which could not be removed. This companion was ever present, ever painful. Like a stake it held him back, prohibiting him from offering his life and his energies to the full.

Some suggest it was the group of 'spoilers' who arrived in every place where Paul went, creating division and dissension. Others see it as a physical ailment – epilepsy, an eye ailment, a disease or malady causing skin irritation, a sexual temptation, an allergy acquired through his occupation as a tent maker. The exact nature of the 'thorn' will, perhaps, never be known. It brought Paul physical and emotional discomfort. His deep sense of his imperfection caused shame and even seemed to evoke pity or scornful rebuke.

Paul reached deep into the Hebrew tradition to pray, to embrace the darkness, and to accept it as working for good. Paul never claimed to be a super-apostle, despite his unique revelation from God and every other credential. The message and the messenger were none other than the Christ, the Hope of Glory. Paul – 'thorn' and all – was but a weak vessel.

Paul knew that voices that cried 'Master!' today could deny him tomorrow. Chants of 'Hosanna!' can quickly transform into cries of 'Crucify him!'. Hands that threw cloaks on the road where Jesus processed in majesty became instruments of violence and destruction.

One of the saintly bishops, a scholar and brilliant preacher, with whom I worked in Sri Lanka used to pray this William Cowper hymn daily:

Hark my soul, it is the Lord; 'Tis the Saviour hear his word –
Jesus speaks and speaks to me; says Poor Sinner lov'st thou me?
I delivered thee when bound:
and when wounded healed thy wounds,
Sought thee wandering, set thee right:
turned thy darkness into light.
Can a woman's tender care: cease towards the child she bear?
Yes, she may forgetful be: still will I remember thee.
Lord it is my chief complaint: that my love is weak and faint.
Yet I love thee and adore, O for grace to love Thee more.

DISCUSSION

How do we regard the thorns in our own sides – as a church community, and as individuals? How do we seek to have our weaknesses transformed to strengths?

CONFESSION

O Christ,
in whose body was named all the violence of the world,
and in whose memory is contained our profoundest grief,
we lay open to you:
the violence done to us in time before memory
the unremembered wounds that have misshaped our lives;
the injuries we cannot forget and have not forgiven.
The remembrance of them is grievous to us;
the burden of them is intolerable.

We lay open to you:
the violence done in our name in time before memory;
the unremembered wounds we have inflicted;
the injuries we cannot forget and for which we have not been forgiven.
The remembrance of them is grievous to us;
the burden of them is intolerable.

We lay open to you:
those who have pursued a violent knowledge the world cannot forget;
those caught up in violence they have refused to name;
those who have enacted violence which they have not repented.
The remembrance of them is grievous to us;
the burden of them is intolerable.

We lay open to you:
the victims of violence whose only memorial is our anger;
those whose suffering was sustained on our behalf;
those whose continued oppression provides the ground we stand on.
The remembrance of them is grievous to us;

the burden of them is intolerable.

Hear what comfortable words our Saviour Christ says to all who truly turn to God:
Come to me, all you who labour and are heavy-laden, and I will give you rest.
Take my yoke upon you, and learn from me, for I am gentle and lowly in heart,

and you will find rest for your souls.

For my yoke is easy, and my burden is light.

Monday *Day 41*

MY GRACE IS SUFFICIENT

But he said to me, 'My grace is sufficient for you, for power is made perfect in weakness.' So, I will boast all the more gladly of my weaknesses, so that the power of Christ may dwell in me. Therefore I am content with weaknesses, insults, hardships, persecutions, and calamities for the sake of Christ; for whenever I am weak, then I am strong. (2 Corinthians 12:9–10)

Grace is one of the most important words used by Paul. He uses it to denote God's activity of benefit and favour given supremely in Jesus Christ. Grace is associated with thanksgiving, with generosity, with the easy trust in relationship that enables partnership, with forgiveness, and with gifts that characterise the nature of God. Grace dwelled in the believer just as the cloud of God's presence rested on the Ark and on Mount Sinai.

From whence does our sufficiency come? Paul asked this question as he struggled with the dilemmas of one made captive to the gospel. He was prepared to surrender all to the person of Jesus and to the cause of Christ. He believed that he would have been able to serve

God with more zeal and to proclaim the gospel with greater fervour if the 'thorn' were removed. Yet he had to live with it.

We have met Paul's story again and again. Abraham and Sarah were aged and barren. God acted and gave them an inheritance more numerous than the stars. Joseph, the dreamer, was betrayed by his brothers. God acted and Joseph provided for many. The people of Israel were captives of Pharaoh. God acted and an empire fell, and the people were freed. Samson was deceived and abandoned, a spectacle of disgust with his eyes gouged and strength lost. God acted and brought deliverance – 'His hair started to grow again.'

The prophets, the psalmists, the lamenters, the leaders of old all cried out, sang, cajoled, pleaded and threatened, in the hope that the people would turn. God acted and the valley of dry bones breathed with the rattle of life. 'Those who wait on the Lord shall renew their strength: they shall mount up with wings like eagles. They shall run and not be weary: they shall walk and not faint.'

When God acted to bring the Word into the human story, a wisp of a girl was chosen. When the wandering carpenter sought leaders for his movement, twelve characters with little courage followed.

Now as one 'untimely born' God had chosen Saul of Tarsus.

Our sufficiency is from God. When we lose this truth we lose the power of God. When the church forgets its source and sufficiency it plays games but makes no impact that lasts.

DISCUSSION

What does it mean to acknowledge God's grace as all-sufficient? 'My strength is made perfect in your weakness' – share examples of this in your life.

LAMBETH 98: Hymn

One of the hymns chosen for the Lambeth Conference is 'God gives us a future' by Elizabeth Smith. It retells this theme.

> God gives us a future,
> daring us to go
> into dreams and dangers
> on a path unknown.
> We will face tomorrow
> in the Spirit's power,
> we will let God change us,
> for new life starts now.

We must leave behind us
sins of yesterday,
for God's new beginning
is a better way.
Fear and doubt and habit
must not hold us back:
God gives us hope, and insight,
and the strength we lack.

Holy Spirit, teach us
how to read the signs,
how to meet the challenge
of our troubled times.
Love us into action,
stir us into prayer,
till we choose God's life, and
find our future there.

Tuesday **Day 42**

THE SIGN OF A TRUE APOSTLE

The signs of a true apostle were performed among you with utmost patience, signs and wonders and mighty works. How have you been worse off than the other churches, except that I myself did not burden you? Forgive me this wrong! Here I am, ready to come to you this third time. And I will not be a burden, because I do not want what is yours but you; for children ought not to lay up for their parents, but parents for their children. (2 Corinthians 12:12–14)

A sign on a church notice board offered a new twist in its message: If you were arrested for being a Christian, what evidence would there be to convict you? This timely question needs a response, from us as individual believers, and from the church as the community of witnesses for Christ.

The 'foolish' discourse, into which Paul was forced in order to keep the Corinthians from falling prey to those creating dissension, was now completed. Paul then moved onto raising the central issues with the community in advance of his third visit to them.

The marks of an apostle in that period of the church's life included signs, wonders and mighty works. Many in the Corinthian community were keen on staying in this constant state of high surprises. Opponents charged that the marks of a true apostle were missing from Paul. He did not accept patronage as a matter of course. Thus, he had no right to special relationship with the Corinthians. With caustic sarcasm Paul asked to be forgiven for not being a monetary burden. A Jewish proverb reminds us that 'we do not inherit the world from our parents - we borrow it from our children'. A true apostle takes this gift from the next generation seriously.

The true apostle described by Paul knows the centre of the universe is more than a hazy force, a mysterious energy, a coded network of natural laws. At the heart of the universe lies a Love so deep, so profound, so passionate, so providential that it can only be characterised as Father, Parent, Mother, as that energy that brings forth and sustains all life. In Jesus, this Father, Parent, Mother revealed the creative love that energises every particle in this vast emerging universe - revealed as a human person. Captured within the bounds of matter, time and space, the face of God was fully revealed, not in regal power, but in lowly servanthood. The servant of the universe hung tortured and shamed on the brutal instrument of death, the Cross. In that moment of shame, the whole world saw and knew the insurmountable depth and height and extent of the Parent's Love. This love never dies. It is always raised up in glory.

The true apostle is, above all, a mark, a sign of this relationship between us, the created, and God who is Parent; a relationship revealing in Jesus Christ, the One crucified, risen and ascended, that God's love is pro-active.

Paul called the church in Corinth to show forth the mark of the true apostle in their relationships, with one another, and with the world they had borrowed from their children.

God,
beyond time you have gifted us with a knowledge of yourself
that spans all generations.
Give us a faith that is prepared to travel joyfully into the future,
that generations to come may praise you O Christ
as Saviour and Lord.

DISCUSSION

How do we bear the mark of the true apostle in our life as a congregation? How do we know God's creative love? How do we bear the mark of the Cross?

LAMBETH 98: Called to be faithful in a plural world

The fellowship we receive from God calls us to wholeness, includes every aspect of our humanity and is itself a reflection of the divine image in us. Spirituality refers both to our experience of that fellowship and also our path towards God. The diversity in our life today brings Christians into contact with many traditions of spirituality. These may have much to contribute to our practice of prayer. At the same time, our knowledge of ourselves has been enlarged by modern psychological study, which can also be helpful in spiritual formation. Some spiritual practices have also been developed in other religious traditions, or outside formal religious disciplines and experiences. These different traditions present yet another challenge to the churches.

Wednesday ***Day 43***

EVERYTHING WE DO, BELOVED, IS FOR 'BUILDING YOU UP'

I will most gladly spend and be spent for you. If I love you more, am I to be loved less? Let it be assumed that I did not burden you. Nevertheless (you say) since I was crafty, I took you in by deceit. Did I take advantage of you through any of those whom I sent to you? I urged Titus to go, and sent the brother with him. Titus did not take advantage of you, did he? Did we not conduct ourselves with the same spirit? Did we not take the same steps? Have you been thinking all along that we have been defending ourselves before you? We are speaking in Christ before God. Everything we do, beloved, is for the sake of building you up. (2 Corinthians 12:15–19)

One story tells of a rector who was so fed up with hearing of the death of the church that he put the obituary notice in the paper. He set the time for a burial service at the local parish church. The whole community turned up at the appointed hour, some out of curiosity, others with a sense of indignation. They were surprised to find a coffin wheeled in by the local undertaker. The rector read the Prayers for the Dead.

After the service the rector informed the large congregation that they could view the body prior to burial. The lid of the coffin was lifted and people filed past in an orderly fashion. Some returned with a puzzled look on their face, others with a smile. Many looked angry and critical. Inside the coffin he had placed a large mirror. Looking in, each person saw him or herself and those around. In the centre of the mirror were the words: 'If the church is dead or dying, you and I are, too.'

The Corinthian church had gone lukewarm in their relationship with Paul. He calls them to reconsider God's bounteous economy. God is the benefactor. God's mission includes us all. For this, Paul and his co-worker Titus were prepared to give all.

He made his defence before God in this letter, and the Corinthian community have listened in on this conversation. The purpose of his exercise, of all ministry, is to build up and, in the building up, to draw all persons closer to Christ.

Almighty God,
fount of all wisdom, crown of all knowledge;
give us eyes to see and minds to understand your marvellous works,
that we may know you through your handiwork
and use your creations to your glory.

DISCUSSION

What signs of life are present in the life of our local church? How is each of us part of that life? How does the Cross, the sign of death in our midst, bring us to new life?

LAMBETH 98: Called to live and proclaim the Good News

Jesus reaches out to those who are excluded – those who are told by their society that they are not needed, because they are too young, too poor, too compromised or too sinful.

The gospel is for people with messy lives. It shows clearest when it gathers people whose main experience in life is one of being shut out.

This may be seen in the work of the Dioceses of Northern Argentina and Chile among indigenous people; in the L'Arche communities with people suffering learning disabilities; in the advocacy and empowerment work of the National Guidance and Empowerment Network of People Living with HIV/AIDS in Uganda. While Good News for the poor is disturbing for those who are comfortable and self-confident, the Good News is offered to those who are materially well off but are searching for community and meaning in their lives. The gospel speaks to that part of *each one of us* that is denied or excluded. Understanding mission involves us in continually letting what is hidden or half-forgotten or rejected in us be brought into the light of Christ.

Inclusion in the community is not the same as inclusiveness for its own sake. To be brought out of isolation or exclusion is to be brought into a relationship with Christ and others that will challenge and transform, into a process that will restructure individual lives and communities.

Inclusion in the community is not a simple process that happens all at once. It needs patience and discernment; and, often, the community has to think about how its structures and practices and even its worship can be an obstacle to the outreach of Jesus. Bringing people in must mean more than just insisting that they fall in with how we do and organise things.

Mission itself changes and renews the church. It can never be reduced to a technique for church growth. Part of our task at Lambeth is to look hard at how the structures of the church work (or fail to work) for renewal through the experience of mission.

Maundy Thursday **_Day 44_**

IS JESUS CHRIST IN YOU?

Examine yourselves to see whether you are living in the faith. Test yourselves. Do you not realise that Jesus Christ is in you? – unless, indeed, you fail to meet the test! (2 Corinthians 13:5)

A recent newspaper article suggested that the elements of the Eucharist, bread and wine, could be available in individual 'take away' packs! You could order the sacrament and some ingenious church organisation could provide a delivery service! There would be no need to worship with the rest of the Christian community.

Paul asked the Corinthians to examine themselves to see if they were living in the faith. The test is, 'Does Jesus Christ live in you?' Has your mind, heart and will been turned to know the thoughts, feelings and actions of Christ? It must show in how you live and act towards each other. If this striving in grace was taking place, Paul's authenticity as leader would not be in question. He had, in fact, kept the faith, and 'run the race' in the gospel. The nature of the community and those whom it brings to Christ divulge the quality of the leader, the minister!

What an awesome test for the whole people of God – those baptised in the Holy Name and marked with the Cross of Christ. They are the Light of Christ in the world. Does Jesus live in you? If not, how can you discover the Christ who lives in the other?

No 'fast food' delivery of the gospel will suffice. Dwelling with God requires time and space, to be and to become. The joyful truth of the gospel is that:

- Jesus Christ the living word takes up residence in us.
- Jesus Christ the living bread takes up living in us.

This is the test: 'Christ in us; the hope of glory'. For those ordained into the sacred ministry who preach the Word and preside over the community in the sacrament of the Lord's Supper, the examination is daunting. In *A Prayer Book for Australia* the admonition given to the priest prior to ordination could not be more direct:

> Remember that you will be called to give account before Jesus Christ: if it should come about that the church, or any of its members, is hurt or hindered as a result of your negligence, you know the greatness of the fault and the judgment that will follow. Therefore apply yourself with diligence and care; and fashion your life and ministry in accordance with Christ's example.

The New Zealand equivalent is similar:

> Serve patiently and cheerfully, remembering that the work you are called to do is God's work; it is in God's hand, and it is done in God's name to God's glory.
>
> Follow Christ whose servant you are. Share the burden of those whose cross is heavy. You are marked as a person who proclaims that among the truly blessed are the poor, the troubled, the powerless, the persecuted.
>
> You must be prepared to be what you proclaim. Serve Christ simply and willingly, and let your joy in Christ overcome all discouragement.
>
> Have no fear; be humble and full of hope.

Those ordained to the sacred orders of the church have an awesome responsibility that can only be fulfilled by prayerful examination and constant encouragement.

Eternal and Holy God, the heavens cannot contain you for your glory exceeds all bounds,
yet you choose us to reveal your love.
Grant to your church a vision of your greatness and a knowledge of your goodness
that your Word may be proclaimed with boldness
and your love portrayed in joyful service,
through Christ our Lord.

DISCUSSION

How do you discern the Christ who lives in others? Does Jesus live in you? Do you seek to give that Christ away?

LAMBETH 98: Called to full humanity

The 19th and 20th centuries have seen developments in technology which have had immense effects upon societies throughout the world. Sometimes these effects have been seen as beneficial and sometimes as highly destructive. Changes in agricultural and manufacturing technology have resulted in populations shifting from rural to urban environments. Work has shifted first from agriculture to manufacturing, and then from manufacturing to service and leisure, often associated with high unemployment and/or part-time employment. 'Liberation' became 'destruction': many people were first redeployed and then unemployed.

Technology has also brought striking changes in communication, but again with positive and negative effects. High speed travel, telephones, television and now the Internet, have allowed people to communicate more easily across the globe. On the negative side, however, the resulting globalisation has often appeared destructive of local cultures. For example, television networks such as CNN have become so dominant in many parts of the world that there is a resulting transfer of the network's own values to the rest of the world.

Globalisation, through technology, can also be a source of increasing division between rich and poor. In addition, technology has enabled scientists to develop ever more destructive weapons, including conventional, nuclear and germ-based. If some believe that these are necessary to maintain peace in the world, others fear that collectively they have made the world even more dangerous.

Finally, the startling developments in biotechnology that have resulted from genetic science in the last two decades suggest the prospect of enormous changes in agriculture and in the treatment of human disease and incapacity. Many fear that these biotechnological developments will also bring negative as well as positive changes, reducing bio-diversity, risking harmful mutations and manipulating human destinies. Biotechnology could be as potentially destructive for future generations as the development of nuclear weapons.

Good Friday ***Day 45***

FOR THE TRUTH

I hope you will find out that we have not failed. But we pray to God that you may not do anything wrong – not that we may appear to have met the test, but that you may do what is right, though we may seem to have failed. For we cannot do anything against the truth, but only for the truth. (2 Corinthians 13:6–8)

The devil was seen dropping pieces of truth on the road. 'Why did you do that?' queried a passer-by. 'You are an enemy of the truth.' 'Well,' replied the devil, 'this is the easiest way of being against the truth. The people who pick up these pieces will surround them with doctrines and dogmas, build shrines to them, fight for them, destroy and kill, and they will forget that at the centre of Truth is Love.'

Once a person in search of Truth discovered a Truth Shop. 'Just what I need,' she said. 'I can now purchase the truth over the counter.' The manager was extremely cooperative. Truth was sold in small portions. No, they did not sell the whole Truth. Exasperated the woman cried out, 'Where can I find the truth for God's sake?!'

'Well, if you must bring God into the picture, I hear that, to find God's truth, you must travel to a place where there is a figure hanging on a cross. Odd, I know, but it's God's truth!'

Paul reiterated to the Corinthians that the test of his authenticity as an apostle was whether they lived out the gospel in word and action. Discipleship affects all of life. In *Window on the Cross,* John V. Taylor speaks of this truth when he says:

> The cross of Jesus Christ cannot be observed objectively from a position of detachment. To be there at all is to be involved, implicated one way or another ... Our whole existence may become involved, since there is no part of it which is untouched by this event.
>
> The true perspective of our lives is not the small, moderate bourgeois world that we pretend is ours but a cosmic stage on which the great extremes of the gospel are stark realities – light and darkness, life and death, luxury and starvation, heaven and perdition.
>
> In this struggle of immense opposites the cross of Jesus Christ towers to its true height.

To stand for the truth, says Paul, is to stand exposed, naked, offered up for all to see. It is to experience the Cross. The Truth that saves is the one that affects every aspect of life – past, present and future – 'We proclaim Christ crucified, a stumbling block to Jews and foolishness to Gentiles but to those who are called – Christ the power of God and the wisdom of God!'

When I survey the wondrous cross
on which the Prince of Glory died
my richest gain I count but loss,
and pour contempt on all my pride.

Were the whole realm of nature mine,
that were an offering far too small:
love so amazing, so divine
demands my life, my soul, my all.

Isaac Watts (1674–1748)

DISCUSSION

Pilate asked 'What is truth?' How is the Cross the eternal mark of truth for all? How do we accept the truth of the Cross as the key to life? How well do we accept the human reality of standing before death on God's Friday?

In *Weep not for me,* John V. Taylor writes:

> But we shall not really become involved in the Passion of Jesus unless we also are willing to be involved more deeply in our world. And when I say 'more deeply', I mean we must learn to see the sufferings of the hungry and oppressed and powerless in the light of this crucifixion. For that is the true mystery of the Cross. Here every human suffering and every human evil is focused into one single event – the dying of the Son of God. As the light and warmth of the sun spread across the landscape is concentrated through a lens to produce one point of intense heat, so in the Cross of Jesus we see all the wrong and injustice of the long human story, all the agonies and griefs of the human race, focused in upon this one sufferer: the Lamb of God who carries the sin of the world. Here is the meaning of it all. Here is the truth of it all. Here is the way through it all and the promise of ultimate salvation.

LAMBETH 98: Called to live and proclaim the Good News

The Good News addresses the sense older people have of being useless and forgotten. In many countries old people can feel neglected and rejected, especially if they have outlived their economic usefulness. In Kenya the model of the church as family proclaims the Good News that everyone has a place; that the old are needed to pass on experience and advice to the young. In Malaysia the Anglican Church has developed senior citizens' clubs, 'Keenager Fellowships' where older people minister to older people, to enable them to have a vision to reach out to their peers and to nurture their grandchildren. In Britain, retired Members of the Mothers' Union can be found spending time visiting men in high security prisons.

> The communication of the gospel ... is the work of local Christian communities who patiently articulate to others what Christ is doing so obviously in their own collective life ... walking in the footsteps of their Master, [they] must be prepared to be buried – buried in a world of cruelty, poverty, bigotry, violence, hopelessness ... the same world which crucified their Master. The church that seeks security, prestige and worldly power is no longer the church of the crucified Jesus. (Vinod Ramachandra, *The recovery of mission* (Carlisle: Paternoster, 1996), 276–277.)

Holy Saturday **Day 46**

BECOME PERFECT

For we rejoice when we are weak and you are strong. This is what we pray for, that you may become perfect. So I write these things while I am away from you, so that when I come, I may not have to be severe in using the authority that the Lord has given me for building up and not for tearing down. (2 Corinthians 13:9–10)

A journalist interviewing Archbishop Tutu during the crisis days in South Africa was surprised to find over the archbishop's study the words: 'Be patient – God has not finished with me yet'.

Paul had a single purpose in his letter to the church in Corinth. He wanted them to experience a change in the right direction, to show an improvement, to evidence a mending of their ways, to experience a renewal. The Greek word translated 'building up' referred to restoring what is broken, be it nets, bones or character. Paul knew the Creation story in the Talmud. The refrain 'and God saw that it was good' is missing on the second day of Creation, when the waters were parted. The Talmud describes the waters at the bottom arguing with the angels and God, wanting to be at the top of creation. The universe is permeated with beauty but it is flawed. It groans, yearns to be restored. The death of Christ had touched all life. The work of the new creation was underway.

Paul had experienced such restoration in Christ. Perfection in every aspect of the Christian character was still far off. But it was being renewed daily into the likeness of the 'new creation' in Christ.

This restoration, this building up in Christ, had given Paul authority. It was an authority that was based on a new pattern of living. It was not based on the Greeks' dependence on perfect knowledge or on the Jewish understanding of perfect law – it was authority from a Cross.

Beware of authority that believes it is 'mistake free' is Paul's plea. When I was elected Bishop of Waikato in New Zealand in 1986 I thought that the decision was a big mistake. I informed a friend about these feelings, and his response put things into perspective for me. 'It could be a mistake,' he pondered. 'So what? God has lived with his mistakes – you and me – for ages. The main issue is, can you learn to live with your mistakes – for there will be many!'

Paul was aware of his own imperfection. He realised that his authority and the decisions that resulted from his leadership could never be described as 'infallible'. What mattered was that the authority being exercised was informed and fashioned by the vision of God's glory found in the face of Jesus Christ.

Eternal Creator,
you have brought us into being, you are aware of our deepest flaws.
In your Christ we rejoice in what we are being made into –
your sons and daughters, children of your eternal becoming.

DISCUSSION

As we wait for the Resurrection on this Holy Saturday, do we also wait in patience for our own perfecting? Do we know Christ hallowing the tomb of our sinfulness to bring us to life? How do we experience the continual process of 'being made new' in Christ?

LAMBETH 98: Called to live and proclaim the Good News

The Great Commission of Matthew 28 to baptise and make disciples is not given to a few specialists, but to all who were gathered in the presence of the risen Christ. The whole church, the assembly summoned by God, is sent with and in Christ, in the power of Christ's resurrection. This is why we must think very hard indeed about how all God's people are to be equipped for mission. The people of God are principally equipped by the gifts of the Holy Spirit and there is renewed awareness of their power in the church today. One implication worth noting is that Christian mission is always a mutual service within the church as well as outreach beyond it; it cannot ever be identified simply with the flow of resources from the privileged to the underprivileged.

If being baptised means being drawn into God's own act of mission, then that divine mission is going on in all of us constantly. The more we let this divine action through, in our plans, words and acts, the more it will achieve its purpose. God's Word does not return empty but accomplishes its purpose. Hence we can say, with Paul, that the One who calls is faithful, and that the One who calls equips us with what we need; and we can rely on the promise of Jesus, as he sends his followers on his business, that he will be with them always.

Called to full humanity

Nowhere do Anglicans live in isolation. They live in neighbourhoods. Their daily lives intersect with and are affected by the lives of others who belong to other faiths. The religious plurality in the midst of which we live and move and have our being obliges the church to relate to other faith communities. Some Anglicans live among Islamic, Hindu and Buddhist communities. In much of the world, Christians suffer the widespread denial of human rights based on religious discrimination. We note the rise of militant fundamentalist religious communities all over the world. Christians must be careful not to descend into counter-fundamentalism. In many such situations, where possible it is important to seek to understand the faith of our neighbours in order to enter into meaningful dialogue with them and to work together for peace and wellbeing in our communities.

Easter Sunday — ***Day 47***

FAREWELL; AND GREET EACH OTHER WITH A HOLY KISS.

Finally, brothers and sisters, farewell. Put things in order, listen to my appeal, agree with one another, live in peace; and the God of love and peace will be with you. Greet one another with a holy kiss. All the saints greet you. (2 Corinthians 13:11–12)

A visit to a *marae* (a meeting place) in Aotearoa New Zealand is a powerful experience. The call of the women elders draws you from one womb of beginning to another. You never arrive alone, for around you are the feathers that support you in your journey keeping you warm. Then comes silence as you remember the ancestors, all in the photograph album of your memory, and any whose snaps are missing. Next there are speeches, truth spoken with clarity so that the winds might carry them from heart to heart. Songs intersperse the speeches to give the spoken word a rhythmic blessing.

The *koha* or gift is offered and received. The formal greeting of each person takes place with the touching of noses twice. It reminds us that the air each inhales comes from the same source. Finally it is time for the Feast. More speeches, songs, dance follows, and then all say farewell. A haunting song accompanies the one who must travel on. 'Now is the hour when we must say goodbye. When you return you'll find me waiting here.'

Henri Nouwen described several meetings with a young person called John who wanted to know Jesus. The time came for him to return to college. 'Will we meet again?' asked John. 'Yes,' replied Henri Nouwen, 'we will, today and to eternity, for, in our discovering together of Jesus, the ground between us, no matter how far we travel, will now be Holy Ground.'

In Jesus Christ, crucified, risen, ascended and glorified, God has kissed the earth. God has touched our nostrils again, breathing into us grace, love and the ever-present partnership of Christ's Spirit. The whole earth, with all of its beauty and ugliness, its wonder and tragedy, its sacrifice and meanness, is declared Holy Ground.

So my friends, it is time for us, who have travelled in study, prayer and reflection over these last few weeks, to say farewell.

My journey in the Christian Way has been one of real surprises. It has led my family into many lands. We have been called to new experiences of God, of the church and of varied avenues for witness and service.

From small village churches with mud walls and thatched roof, to glorious cathedrals resplendent with stained glass windows and marble arches, I have been strengthened by the faithful witness of those whose lives have been fashioned by the Christ of the Cross and Resurrection.

One such witness was Kylie, a 9-year-old victim of polio that had paralysed her, leaving her on a stretcher-like chair. She attended church regularly. She was one of those real encouragers who was able to put people at ease; friendly and engaging. On every occasion I visited the parish, Kylie would wait for her chance to meet with me – a smile, a word of encouragement, and then the inevitable sadness as the time of goodbyes came. She was a vibrant, dynamic being, full of grace and joy, held in a body that was taut and twisted.

One night, just before Easter, Kylie took very ill and within a matter of hours she was dead. Kylie had been prepared to die – for Resurrection had been a part of her everyday life.

Her funeral service brought in hundreds of people. Her life had touched so many. The children placed flowers on her coffin as her favourite hymn was sung:

He came singing love,
He lived singing love,
He died singing love,
He rose in silence.

For His love to go on
We must make it our song,
You and I be the singers.

I thank God this day, for in Christ's grace I belong to a wonderful community – the Resurrection People whose song is 'Alleluia!'

Glorious Lord of Life,
we praise you,
that by the mighty resurrection of your Son,
you have delivered us from sin and death
and made your whole creation new;
grant that we who celebrate with joy
Christ's rising from the dead
may be raised from the death of sin
to the life of righteousness;
through him who lives and reigns with you and the Holy Spirit,
one God now and for ever.
Living Christ, you are risen from the dead!
Love reigns!
You are life stronger than death;
raise our eyes to see you
as the new day dawns.

DISCUSSION

How will we declare 'Christ is Risen!' in our world? How can we know that in Christ all ground, all life, is truly Holy Ground?

LAMBETH 98: Called to full humanity

Anglicans have made great contributions to peace-making in many parts of the world. Some have been martyred. We think of the martyrdom of the late Ugandan Archbishop Janani Luwum, and the faithful witness of Archbishop George Browne at the height of the civil war in Liberia. We also recognise the prophetic witness of Archbishop Desmond Tutu in opposition to apartheid in South Africa. Today, we acknowledge the peace efforts of the Anglican bishops in Jerusalem and in Ireland. There are examples of Anglicans witnessing to racial justice in North America and Britain and who are active in defusing conflicts. Anglicans make their contribution within the context of a world anxious for lasting peace. The World Council of Churches has inaugurated the Programme to Combat Violence, a renewed challenge to churches to be sacrificially engaged in active peace-making. We need to continue to develop non-violent methods of struggle for peace and justice within a framework of democracy.

In *Jesus rediscovered* Malcolm Muggeridge described Jesus as:

> A man, who was born and lived like us; whose presence and teaching have continued to shine for generation after generation ... A man who died, but who none the less, in some quite unique way, remained, and remains, alive. A man who offered us the mysterious prospect of dying in order to live; who turned all the world's values upside down, telling us that it was the weak, not the strong, who mattered, the simple, not the learned, who understood, the poor, not the rich, who were blessed ...
>
> And now? Well, all I can say is, as one ageing and singularly unimportant fellow man, that I have conscientiously looked far and wide, inside and outside my own head and heart, and I have found nothing other than this man and his words which offers any answer to the dilemmas of this tragic, troubled time. If his light has gone out, then, as far as I am concerned, there is no light.

BIBLIOGRAPHY

Barnett, Paul, *The message of 2 Corinthians* (Leicester: IVP, 1988).

Bonhoeffer, Dietrich, *Letters and papers from prison* (Great Britain: Collins, 1966).

Brugemann, Walter, *The prophetic imagination* (USA: Fortress Press, 1978).

Carey, George, *The great 'God' robbery* (London: Fount, 1989).

Coggan, Donald, *The prayers of the New Testament* (London: Hodder and Stoughton, 1967).

Craven, Margaret, *I heard the owl call my name* (London: Picador, 1974).

Diocese of Newcastle, *Come listen live* (Newcastle: 1997).

Douglas-Klotz, Neil, *Prayer of the cosmos* (New York: HarperCollins, 1995).

Holloway, Richard, *The stranger in the wings* (Great Britain: SPCK, 1994).

Lewis, C. S., *The four loves* (Great Britain: Fontana, 1963).

Muggeridge, Malcolm, *Jesus rediscovered* (Great Britain: Collins/Fontana, 1969).

Oestreicher, Paul, *The double cross* (London: Darton, Longman and Todd, 1986).

Ramachandra, Vinod, *The recovery of mission* (Carlisle: Paternoster, 1996).

Taylor, John V., *Weep not for me* (Geneva: WCC, 1986).

Trible, Phyllis, *God and the rhetoric of sexuality* (Philadelphia: Fortress Press, 1978).

Witherington, Ben III, *Conflict and community in Corinth* (USA: Eerdmans, 1995).

Young, Frances and Ford, David, *Meaning and truth in 2 Corinthians* (Great Britain: SPCK, 1987).